Stagflation

Stagflation

**The Penalty of Speculative Production
in a Multistage Economy**

Eric D. Bovet

LexingtonBooks

D.C. Heath and Company
Lexington, Massachusetts
Toronto

Library of Congress Cataloging in Publication Data
Bovet, Eric D. (Eric David), 1900–
Stagflation, the penalty of speculative production in a multistage economy.

 Bibliography: p.
 Includes index.
 1. Unemployment—Effect of inflation on.
2. Economics. 3. Profit. 4. Prices. I. Title
II. Title: Speculative production in a multistage economy.
HD5710.B68 1983   339.5   82-48021
ISBN 0-669-05883-1

Published simultaneously in Canada

Printed in the United States of America

International Standard Book Number: 0-669-05883-1

Library of Congress Catalog Card Number: 82-48021

To the Memory of Wesley C. Mitchell,
Under Whose Aegis This All Got Started

Contents

Contentsix

Foreword

The presentation of a new idea or analytical approach is cause for excitement among professionals in any field. In this book, Dr. Bovet has provided economists with an interesting and highly stimulating line of thinking about the underlying causes of stagflation. Included, also, are his practical suggestions for dealing more effectively with this disturbing phenomenon, which afflicts contemporary developed capitalistic countries.

Dr. Bovet has taken a structural approach and has tied the occurrence of stagflation to the process of production and the speculative pattern of decision making that this imposes upon individual producers at each stage in the production chain. It is his thesis that, in a multistage economy, a number of unavoidable hazards accompany production and pricing decisions made well in advance of knowing what demand conditions for the output will be when it finally rolls off the line.

One obvious danger Dr. Bovet considers is the erroneous expectations and predictions that preclude both optimum consumer service and maximum corporate profits. Another much more subtle and more treacherous hazard, he points out, is the impact of anticipatory production and distribution on the operation of the price mechanism. The various obstacles that impede the relay of price changes from market to market, vertically speaking, directly interfere with the equation of supply and demand. This inevitably produces inefficiency in all business dealings.

In addition, by preventing price changes from being communicated promptly to each stage, the speculative-production arrangement results in imperfectly balanced profit margins at successive stages. The ultimate consequence, Dr. Bovet concludes, can only be stagflation and inflation, the conditions of stagflation. Required for improved functioning of industries and the economy is an immediate and accurate transmission of price changes to all stages of the production process.

This is a serious problem since, even if predictions of consumer demand were always correct, the inherent inefficiencies of the structure would continue to result in a deterioration in consumer service as well as in business profits.

Dr. Bovet's thesis is carefully reasoned, and his argument is fully developed. He has presented a challenge to the profession, and it is incumbent upon those who are skeptical to prove any lack of validity of his case through logical argument and empirical studies.

Having developed his explanation of the stagflation phenomenon, Dr. Bovet goes on to suggest practical measures for dealing with the problem. It would not be fair to the author to reveal too much in this foreword. The reader will have to explore the book for the cure offered for this disturbing contemporary economic problem.

Whether the author's analysis of the problem and his proposed solutions will stand the test of time and careful professional scrutiny remains to be seen. In the meantime, economists should be grateful to Dr. Bovet for having opened a novel and stimulating line of thought.

William P. Snavely
Professor of Economics,
George Mason University

Preface and Acknowledgments

In this book, I introduce a somewhat novel approach to economics. Some of the more obstinate problems, such as stagnation and instability, are attacked from an unfamiliar angle. In the text, it is claimed that the new thinking is just an extension of the mainstream of economic theory.

Much of the new approach is in line with existing theory; but certain features are clear departures from traditional concepts:

1. Elements representing extensions of the mainstream of economic thought:

   Study of chains of transactions through the channels of alternating stages and markets;

   Study of the price system as a self-adjusting mechanism for supply and demand as these travel through the pipeline;

   Study of the price system as a mechanism allocating and equilibrating profit margins at successive stages;

   Study of the impact of speculative production and distribution on the efficiency of the price system in a multistage economy (for the above elements see chapter 3); and

   Study of how distorted profit margins generate economic entropy, that is, the gap between the nation's production capacity and the effective demand, as well as stagflation (see chapter 4).

2. Elements representing departures from the mainstream of economic thought:

   Shift from empirical observation to the formulation of hypotheses (see chapter 2);

   Elaboration of a non-Euclidean theory of value (see chapter 5); and

   Development of a generalized system of economic thought (see chapter 6).

The reader may wish to refer to the above framework as he progresses through the pages of part I.

In part II, some recommended remedies consist of going back into history to a period before the Industrial Revolution, when unemployment and business cycles were unknown. Present outdated marketing practices were safe and efficient in the atmosphere of the Golden Age, before the advent of vertical specialization and speculative production (see chapter 8).

Other remedies take us into the future, when our incompatible marketing practices are revamped and adapted for use in a modern industrial, speculative, multistage economy (see chapter 9).

Either approach should help escape from the clutches of stagflation, that relentless affliction of the 1980s.

Several distinguished economists offered valuable comments on the manuscript of this book. They contributed to the historical accuracy, internal consistency, and expository clarity of the text. Their suggestions helped make the book more readable. The reviewers included Charles W. Howe, professor of economics, University of Colorado, Boulder, and visiting professor, the Rockefeller Foundation, University of Yogyakarta, Indonesia; Robert A. Leone, professor of Economics and lecturer in public policy, John F. Kennedy School of Government, Harvard University; and William P. Snavely, professor of economics and associate dean, College of Arts and Sciences, George Mason University, Fairfax, Virginia. I owe sincere gratitude to these eminent scholars for their help.

Introduction:
Political and Economic
Roots of Stagflation

My intent in this book is to discuss the economic aspects of stagflation. Stagflation, however, is not a purely economic phenomenon. On the contrary, the political overtones have become so predominant that we must sort out the respective shares of political and economic impacts.

It has been claimed that stagflation would be impossible in an ideal, fully competitive economy. Wage rates would gradually decline, so the reasoning goes, to a point where the jobless would be absorbed on existing or new payrolls. Monetary restraints could then safely be applied to counteract inflation. I agree with this view, provided that the ideal economy is also a nonspeculative one. In an actual situation, even with full competition, there would still be inefficiencies resulting from speculative production that would preclude full employment and stable prices.

With regard to the ideal, fully competitive economy, two main obstacles stand in its way. One obstacle is purely economic, pertaining to competitive pressures underlying price and wage rigidities, as well as the propensity to seek monopolistic protection. The other obstacle is political: acts of Congress conferring special privileges upon certain groups. Among the acts are the minimum-wage laws (since 1938), which harm the chances of the young and minority groups to find employment; agricultural price supports and output restrictions; the Davis-Bacon Act, which requires excessive wages to be paid under government contracts; many privileges granted to workers and especially to labor unions; unemployment and related benefits high enough to finance strikes and discourage work; and import tariffs that subsidize inefficient domestic industries. The cumulative effect of these exceptions to the rule of free competition is sufficient to hamstring the important levers of the economy to a point where stagflation is invited.

Two additional political roots of stagflation were born of fear. The first was a paradox: the fear of unemployment. The joblessness of the Great Depression of the 1930s was protracted and devastating. A repetition after World War II had to be averted at all costs. The Employment Act of 1946 squarely placed on the U.S. government the mandate to assure employment for the greatest number. Keynes' *General Theory,* born before the war, was beginning to sway Washington's economists. To stimulate aggregate demand, government projects were escalated, and a conservative rate of inflation of 3 percent per annum was believed desirable.

Keynesian premises militated against retiring the public debt, subjecting the nation to the possibility of insolvency if another major depression or yet another world war were to strike. Politicians reveled in the new atmosphere.

They enjoyed the power conferred on legislators by the creeping tax-bracket syndrome, which guaranteed automatic increases in government revenues.

Had the administration been mindful of unemployment's twin problem, business cycles, it might have adopted a countercyclical policy of boosting employment during periods of stagnation and reducing the debt in prosperous times. As it was, the government ended up stimulating the demand during twenty-five years of prosperity.

All went well, even through the years of the Vietnam war and the oil crisis, although the national debt was more than doubled in less than ten years, until the advent of stagflation. Economists have now learned that the yield of the multiplier does have limits and that these are uncomfortable to live with. The nation is faced with painful withdrawal symptoms from its thirty-five-year experiment with a managed economy and finds it distasteful to have to relinquish erstwhile amenities now considered necessities. Thus it was the fear of unemployment that, using the Keynesian recipe, led to political excesses in improvident disregard of America's future.

Another political root of stagflation was the fear of the spread of communism. The fear manifested itself after the end of World War II not only in the U.S. intervention in South Korea and Vietnam but also in a shift of the U.S. government toward the political left. This implied a trend toward socialization of certain functions, including an expansion of social security and countless other benefits, under the aegis of the federal government. Unfortunately the government overextended itself; the net result has been a weakening rather than a strengthening of capitalism. Thus a fear of the spread of communism has also contributed to precipitate stagflation.

This leaves little room in which to maneuver. It seems paramount that the U.S. government reduce the cost of servicing the debt, balance budgets, and amortize the debt. These goals could have been achieved easily during the twenty-five years of prosperity. Now they must be reached at the cost of high unemployment.

The economic roots of stagflation are described in this book. Stagflation is a combination of stagnation and inflation. Inflation and its antagonist, deflation, may be covered by the term *economic instability*. Thus stagnation and instability are the economic roots of stagflation. These have not been fully explained in the economic literature. The explanation presented in chapters 3 and 4 consists of an analysis of the mainspring of all economic endeavor, the profit motive. For that reason, the explanation is called the *profit-motive theory of unemployment and business cycles*.

Considering that the profit motive is the most potent force known in economics, it is surprising that not more attention has been devoted to its study. If that energy is found not to be fully utilized in a modern economy, it would seem opportune to investigate the possibilities of releasing a greater proportion of it for the benefit of producers and consumers.

The analysis begins by asking three questions: (1) What are the requisites for the profit motive to induce efficient behavior on the part of the entrepreneur? (2) Are these requisites fulfilled in a speculative multistage economy? (3) What needs to be done in order for the profit motive to induce optimal decisions for the firm as well as for society as a whole? These three questions require, before they can be answered, an in-depth study of how profit margins are determined, whether they are determined efficiently, and if not, why not?

Eventually the investigator must question the price mechanism as the lever determining profit margins. The price mechanism is said to have its flaws. Its more obvious task is to equate supply and demand, and it may not accomplish that task with the desired promptness and accuracy. But another task, much more essential and critical than the first, consists of setting profit margins at successive stages of vertical marketing channels. Unfortunately the price mechanism may fail to perform that function dependably, with confusion and inefficiency the inevitable outcome. If profit margins are distorted from balanced levels, consecutive firms in the pipeline, which seek to maximize profits that have become garbled, will be induced to operate at cross-purposes, generating chronic waste. The waste and other inefficiencies may eventually cumulate into economic stagnation and instability.

Unemployment and business cycles may be ascribed to the distortion of profit margins through the partial paralysis of the price mechanism, for the price mechanism may not be able to operate effectively in a speculative multistage economy. It may be concluded that a speculative multistage economy is saddled with an economic entropy, which makes for a variety of inefficiencies such as stagflation, an entropy that would be unknown in a nonspeculative economy.

That conclusion bears out a suspicion I had over forty years ago that speculative production might harm a multistage economy (even when all predictions are always accurate and profits always maximized) by interfering with the free operation of the price mechanism and its important profit-margin balancing function. Had it not been for that suspicion, which quite unexpectedly turned out to be relevant, it might have been almost impossible to stumble on the hidden, underlying microeconomic factors affecting such macroeconomic phenomena as stagnation and unemployment, instability and business cycles, the economic roots of stagflation.

The speculative-production hypothesis furnished the hinge between a healthy, stable, and efficient economy (an abstract nonspeculative one) and our limping economy (a real speculative one). It yielded a first inkling of what we may try to do if we hope to avoid harmful consequences.

The economic entropy is a malaise that underlies every facet of economic activity. It manifests itself in a wide variety of disorderly processes. If the suspicion that led to the discovery of economic entropy is borne out, nonspeculative production, or its equivalent, could be the theoretical answer to a number of economic problems.

Indeed excessive competitive pressure cannot be eliminated without recuperating wasted purchasing power, and the latter cannot be fully recovered without unemployment disappearing. Again consumer demand cannot be fulfilled efficiently unless inventories are stabilized, and inventories cannot be steadied unless business cycles vanish. All of these symptoms have a common origin. If the origin of a single symptom can be understood and appropriate precautionary measures taken, all may subside as a result of identical policies.

Speculative production and distribution cannot help generating the symptoms. Structural incompatibilities inevitably stand in the way of efficient performance. There is a necessary cause-and-effect relationship between the antecedent (speculative production) and the consequence (modern economic ills).

What are the opportunities for reversing the process, for bringing about economic prosperity and stability by avoiding speculative production? No one knows the answer to that question. We have no empirical examples of such recoveries taking place, except that before the Industrial Revolution, the economic entropy had not yet set in. What could reasonably be argued today is that since speculative production is deleterious to the economy, it might be worthwhile avoiding it to see what would happen. It would seem sensible to investigate ways of preventing speculative production or the processes it controls. Part II of the book discusses such possibilities.

Let me illustrate. Whereas the explanation of a growth phenomenon is usually multiple, that of a stoppage of growth may well be single. In order for the daisy to bloom, it needs earth, moisture, chemicals, air, heat, light. In order for the daisy to wilt, only a drought is needed—the lack of one of the elements necessary to its growth: moisture. Similarly, a living organism such as an economy requires a number of factors to keep healthy. The lack of a single element—for example, the efficient operation of the price mechanism—may explain the malaise or entropy that manifests itself as unemployment and business cycles. Restoring economic efficiency and health can be achieved theoretically through a single remedy—nonspeculative production—or its equivalent. But its practical application remains and will always remain an art.

A brief explanation of the book's subtitle is warranted. The term *speculative production* is defined as the well-established practice of producing for stock rather than waiting for customer orders. As used here, speculative production is synonymous with *anticipatory production*. In this book, speculative production includes speculative distribution or the anticipation of consumer wants by making finished goods available on retail shelves.

The opposite of speculative production (and distribution) is production (and distribution) to order. The title states that speculative production in a multistage or vertically specialized economy has for its penalty the phenomenon of stagflation, a superimposition of inflation upon stagnation. The economic value of anticipatory production is not disputed. The comparative merits of speculative production versus production to order, just as the merits of vertical specialization versus vertical integration, have been discussed repeatedly in the literature, but their respective impact on the operation of the price mechanism has been of no concern in those discussions. The point made in the first part of this book is that theoretically speculative production has unexpected drawbacks, which may explain important macroeconomic short-comings. With that knowledge, better management techniques perhaps can be designed that may prevent the shortcomings.

Not specified in the subtitle of the book is the content of the second part: the description of possible remedies for avoiding stagflation, with or without speculative production.

Part I
Economic Analysis

This book has two parts. Part I contains economic analysis or theory, an explanation of the economic roots of stagflation. Part II discusses economic synthesis or reconstruction, a set of recommended business-management policies designed to avoid the economic components of stagflation.

Chapter 1 and 2 show how economic theory has evolved from the early classics to the present time and what opportunities exist for another potential step forward. Chapters 3 and 4 examine how speculative production in a multistage economy may breed inefficient consumer service, stagnation, unemployment, instability, business cycles, and stagflation.

The word *stagflation* is a contraction of *stagnation* and *inflation*. Inflation and its antagonist, deflation, can be designated as instability. When the political aspects of stagflation are removed, the residual economic problem is a twin problem of stagnation and instability. Thus, we are brought back to the still-unresolved problems of unemployment and business cycles. Whoever explains these explains stagflation.

A theory of value appropriate to a speculative economy is submitted in chapter 5; a generalized system of economic thought and an algorithm suitable for modeling a modern industrial economy, in chapter 6.

1 Past Achievements of Economic Theory

The profit-motive theory of unemployment and business cycles, which ascribes stagflation to speculative production in a multistage economy, is best presented against the background of past and existing economic thought. It is not exactly an extension of current trends, yet grows out of the state of the art as it now stands. A brief review of the development of economic theory in this chapter sets the stage for chapter 2, which looks to the future.

Stepwise Progress of Economic Thought

The progress of economic thought over the past four hundred years has not been uniform. It has been wedded to the publications of great individual thinkers, each of whom has pushed the state of the art one notch at a time. This is true of the contributions and assumptions that are of particular interest to the purpose at hand.

Among the many authors representing each school, those selected for analysis here have left an innovative and lasting imprint on subsequent developments. Some have invited, some have retarded, the next step forward.

The Classics

The mercantilists, bent on gold and silver as the substance of wealth, prescribed remedies against rising prices: they advocated international free trade two hundred years before Adam Smith. The physiocrats, who substituted land in their definition of wealth, originated the doctrine of laissez faire.

Adam Smith (1723–1790) believed labor was the sole source of value. For him, labor was the real measure of the exchange value of commodities.

Smith made the first comprehensive statement on price. The real price for him was the toil and trouble of acquiring goods. Since the value of money fluctuates with its production costs and falls when the currency is debased, the money price of goods may stray from their real price. The true price of a commodity includes the true price of all the factors incorporated; however, the actual price at which a commodity is sold is the market price. It may or may not equal the natural price, which Smith defined as the price toward which the market price gravitates in a competitive economy.

The market price is regulated by the quantity brought to market and the effectual demand of those willing to pay the natural price. Competition among buyers tends to increase the price; the proportion of the increase is governed by the importance that buyers attribute to the commodity. Competition among sellers lowers the price, with the degree of the decrease depending on the sellers' anxiousness to get rid of their goods, particularly perishable goods.

A balance of supply and demand is to the interest of all. Where equality is attained, the price covers all costs, all effectual demand is satisfied, and no excess of supply lowers the price. As long as supply and demand tend toward balance, the market price of all commodities continually gravitates toward the natural price.

Adam Smith was well aware of the use by sellers of artificial means to maintain high prices. The limits to production capacity, monopolies, and government intervention, all have a similar influence. Smith was extremely critical of such restraints. In discussing price, he assumed a freely competitive market as the ideal market.

Adam Smith is also credited with the idea that where free competition prevails, every individual is led as by an invisible hand to promote an end that was no part of his intention: the best public interest.

The total contribution made by *The Wealth of Nations* was resounding. Over two hundred years ago, the fundamental principles of political economy were set down scientifically for the first time.

Adam Smith published his treatise before the onset of chronic unemployment and business cycles. While the beginning of the Industrial Revolution in Great Britain is generally set around the middle of the eighteenth century, the incidence of mass unemployment and business cycles did not become manifest until the end of that century, after publication of *The Wealth of Nations*. Adam Smith therefore cannot be held responsible for ignoring these symptoms. His general optimism was warranted. His was the Golden Age that preceded the calamities of industrial economies during the nineteenth and twentieth centuries.

Had Adam Smith lived and written but fifty years later, he might have become alarmed by a turn of events he had not foreseen: the human misery that accompanied the industrialization process in the British Isles. He might have revised some of his fundamental and admirably simple pronouncements. Both his market and price theory and his confident statement concerning the guidance lent by the invisible hand may have been obsolete for 150 years. It may no longer be true that even with freely competitive markets, the market price gravitates toward the natural price or that selfish entrepreneurs promote the best interests of society.

The prestige of *The Wealth of Nations* was so great that Smith's followers passed on to future writers the substance of his faith. A long line of successors —in fact most of the economic authors of the classical and neoclassical school

—followed in his footsteps. They did not ignore the realities of economic stagnation and instability, but while recognizing these ills, they nevertheless were slow in incorporating them into their theories.

Evaluation. Adam Smith's theory, written before the onset of unemployment and business cycles, is inadequate for application to the kind of economy that emerged from the Industrial Revolution—a speculative, multistage economy.

David Ricardo (1772–1823) believed that the power of competition, and it alone, determined the wages of laborers, the profit of entrepreneurs, and the rent of landowners. Holding the labor market to be governed by supply and demand, he concluded that wages tended to equal subsistence wages. Ricardo mirrored the pessimism of Malthus (1766–1834). Ricardo observed the rivalries between labor and management, as well as between landowners and entrepreneurs. These rivalries became exacerbated with the development of machinism and industrialization. Ricardo sided with the entrepreneur.

Evaluation. David Ricardo's views, though less optimistic than those of Adam Smith, still reflect the preindustrial age, when the problems typical of the present era had not yet arisen. His thinking therefore is insufficient to throw light on the origins of modern economic ills.

Jean-Baptiste Say (1767–1832) was still of the opinion that as long as the government did not intervene, the self-regulating mechanism of economic activity tended to ensure overall equilibrium. By formulating his famous law of outlets—that supply creates its own demand—he ruled out the possibility of both unemployment and business cycles. Over the years, Say's Law was held in such high esteem that even today the majority of economists believe it to be true in a barter economy, although it may not be applicable in a money and credit economy.

Evaluation. Like Smith and Ricardo, Say was a son of the Golden Age. As the effects of industrialization made themselves felt, his views ceased to be relevant. However, the reason may have little to do with money and credit.

John Stuart Mill (1806–1873) was born into the nineteenth century. He substituted utilitarian motives for the natural laws of his predecessors and believed that individual happiness is the object of all economic activity.

Evaluation. John Stuart Mill synthesized selected elements of the theories of earlier classics. He did acknowledge the existence of economic depressions, ascribing these to the extension of credit; however, he failed to integrate depressions into his theory, which therefore remained unrealistic.

Challenging the classical theory, Karl Marx (1818–1883) sided with the laborer. This shift can be attributed directly to his observation of the hardships visited on the working classes in England as a result of the Industrial

Revolution: mass unemployment, and trade cycles. Marx described eloquently what he saw: the growing power of landowners and employers, the mergers and concentrations of industrial firms, and the rising indigence of the masses. While Marx recognized technological unemployment resulting from capital improvements and the concentration of industry, he never dealt fully with the origin of unemployment. Nor did he explain the origin of business cycles or the widening cleavage between rich and poor. His unfortunate conclusion was that capitalism was doomed by its contradictions, the only way out being revolution and the shift to a totalitarian socialist regime.
Evaluation. Such betrayal only retarded the problem's resolution. Karl Marx left undone the work in need of accomplishment: the explanation of the prime causes of inefficiency, incomplete utilization of resources, and instability in a capitalist economy.

The Neoclassics

The neoclassical school of economic theory signaled the next important step upward in the ascent to present levels of economic understanding. Léon Walras (1834–1910), a French engineer called to the University of Lausanne, Switzerland, borrowed the concept of marginal utility as the determinant of market price and added the idea of scarcity of the goods. Price expresses quantitatively utility and limited supply. He defended both free competition and laissez faire. He was the first to express economic relations in mathematical language. He concentrated his investigations on the process of price formation on the market and became noted for his theory of exchange.

Finally Walras developed his renowned theory of general economic equilibrium. Markets are of three types, said Walras: the commodity market, the service market, and the producers' goods market. Economic equilibrium requires the simultaneous equation of supply and demand on all three markets. Price changes must be freely transferable between markets. The entrepreneur provides the link. Walras believed that under perfect competition, the overall equilibrium is always attained. In this system, the selling price always equals production costs; there is no residual excess profit.

With the proviso of perfect competition and freely transferable price changes among the three markets, Walras was partially right. But his assumption of freely transferable price changes along vertical marketing channels made the model unrealistic.

Walras's contribution has been extremely useful. His theory has been widely applied and has permitted approximate solutions to many practical problems. Among the criticisms leveled at him are that his is a closed and static system, permitting of no disequilibrium or growth. In actuality, entrepreneurs seek to exploit situations of disequilibrium; by doing so, they accelerate the return to equilibrium.

The notion of general economic equilibrium has been criticized by Joseph A. Schumpeter, by Nicholas Kaldor in "The Irrelevance of Equilibrium Economics," by Joan Robinson in *Economic Heresies,* and others. But no one has been more eloquent in denouncing the shortcomings of the Walrasian model than the Hungarian mathematical economist Janos Kornai in *Anti-Equilibrium.* Kornai was exasperated by the lack of realism, and hence relevance, of general equilibrium as formally presented in mathematical terms by the Arrow-Debreu models.

Kornai's vehement attack lists twelve deficiencies. He charges that general equilibrium is static and stationary, that the Walrasian model is a single-stage model in which producer and consumer meet face to face and there is no subordination, that interstage conflicts are disregarded, and that such a model is unsuitable for the study of multistage control phenomena. I could not agree more, for those were precisely the limitations of the Walrasian model that retarded most the next advance in economic theory. Unfortunately the tremendous popularity of Léon Walras crystallized the thinking of innumerable economists.

Evaluation. Léon Walras reached a plateau considerably higher than that of the classics but not in the direction of realism. His system is still built with the classical view that unemployment is impossible and business cycles non-existent. A single assumption vitiated the validity of his contribution: the assumption that price changes are freely transferable between markets. Walras was concerned only with the transfer of price changes among the commodity market, the service market, and the producers' goods market; he was not preoccupied with the pipeline. The profit-motive theory shows that in a speculative, multistage economy, price changes are not and cannot be freely transferred between vertically aligned markets; hence stagflation results.

Walras was followed, at the University of Lausanne, by the Italian engineer Vilfredo Pareto (1848–1923). Carrying the Walrasian theme one step further, Pareto taught that consumers can satisfy their many wants in a number of different ways. Helpful in making optimum choices as between alternate quantities of alternate merchandise is a set of indifference curves. When both producers and consumers seek to maximize their satisfactions, there exists a system of prices that optimizes all of the choices. This is a situation where it is impossible to modify individual choices without decreasing the well-being of at least one agent. Pareto-optimal choices are still very much utilized in a number of applications. The strongest criticism that can be made is the unrealistic simplification whereby vertical markets are telescoped into a single market.

Pareto-optimality may hold only in a speculative economy subjected to economic entropy. A set of decisions by various agents may be optimal in such an economy, but satisfactions of one or more agents may be increased without anyone else being worse off as soon as the economy is made as efficient as a nonspeculative economy, or its equivalent.

Evaluation. Vilfredo Pareto's contribution prolongs the dimensions of that of Walras but still not in the direction of realism. Theory has not gained altitude from the plateau of general equilibrium theory.

Alfred Marshall (1842–1924) integrated the strongest elements of classical and neoclassical theories into a single, comprehensive pattern. Fascinated by price-formation mechanisms, Marshall established the distinction between short- and long-run phenomena. In the short run, productive capacity is fixed, and output is limited to existing facilities; in the long run, the entrepreneur can vary capital stock and production. This leads Marshall to use two series of cost curves: a limited range of instantaneous costs and a broader range of costs applying to long-run variable investments and variable outputs. Short-run costs are essentially determined by demand since the capital stock is fixed. In the long run, supply costs have the stronger influence.

For Alfred Marshall, a pragmatist, free competition diverges from the perfect competition of earlier economists, which implied perfect knowledge of the market and perfect mobility of the factors of production. In his view, free competition requires only average information and reasonable labor and capital mobility. Marshall detected an element of monopoly in every firm. Depending on the type of enterprise, varying degrees of monopoly should be expected and taken into account. Aware of the imperfections of competition in real life, he nevertheless upheld the merits of a freely competitive market in promoting equilibrium between production and consumption.

Evaluation. For all his breadth and skill, Alfred Marshall did not surpass the unrealistic neoclassical single-stage model. Neither did he facilitate the transition to the next advance in economic theory. He consolidated the status quo.

Business-Cycle Theory before Keynes

Theories that attempted to explain the causes of business cycles proliferated for about forty years beginning at the turn of this century. Since World War II, there has been virtually a complete vacuum in that field. Little new research was initiated, and it seems as though no interest existed in resolving the problem. True, built-in stabilizers and a demand-pushing monetary policy combined to reduce the amplitude of economic fluctuations, and twenty-five years of prosperity placated the mood of researchers. It did mean a long hiatus in serious economic research into the causes of business cycles.

The existence of business cycles has been questioned. Perhaps they are the result of external shocks, the ripples of one shock never having time to die out before the next shock strikes. The periodicity of cycles, short cycles, intermediate cycles, long cycles, has been found to be subject to many irregularities. If the turning points of the cycle are set by constraints within the economy, variations in the amplitude and duration of successive waves should be expected.

Cyclical fluctuations affect a variety of elements of the economic process, among them prices, wages, production and distribution volumes, inventories, interest rates, the rate of growth, and employment levels. Therefore economists have often switched to the more general concept of economic fluctuations, for regardless of their causes, no one disputes their existence. However, the term *business cycles* will be used in this book.

The notion of causality as applied to business cycles needs clarification. Existing business-cycle theory was conceived in an effort to explain the cause or causes of the phenomenon, and the term *cause* is freely used in the majority of texts. It has always been the hope of researchers to come up with an explanation that would furnish the tools necessary to avoid a recurrence. Had any of the theories succeeded, the problem of stagflation would be half-solved. The truth is that much of the theory has been incomplete. What has been brought to light in most instances should be considered as proximate causes, leaving the prime causes still deeply buried.

Much of the existing theory is macroeconomic; that alone may account for the superificiality of the analyses. The key to the problem must be looked for in the microeconomic foundations of macroeconomic phenomena such as business cycles. Furthermore, the majority of the explanations are concerned primarily with money, credit, and investments. Although these undoubtedly play a role in the chain of events that lead to cycles, monetary factors may have nothing to do with the real prime causes. Unless we dig into the mysterious underground, we will forever be talking about business cycles, not revealing their roots. We will leave unanswered the pertinent questions: Why are we plagued by business cycles? What can we do to prevent (not just mitigate) their occurrence?

Nevertheless, business-cycle theory has made a crucial contribution to progress in this area. It has recognized the existence of business cycles steadfastly denied by classical and neoclassical thought, and it has focused attention on many cogent aspects of the problem.

The definitive compendium of business-cycle theory is *Prosperity and Depression* (Haberler 1937). It contains a logical classification of the many theories published during the period in question.

The Purely Monetary Theory. Ralph G. Hawtrey looks to monetary factors as the exclusive cause of business cycles. In an age preceding the onset of chronic inflation, monetary factors consisted primarily of bank credit and secondarily of the volume of currency. The velocity of monetary circulation determines the briskness of business. An expansion of credit signals the ascending phase of the cycle; a contraction signals the descending phase. The wide amplitude of fluctuations is explained by their cumulative and self-reinforcing nature. The cumulative effect reflects the rise or fall in merchants' inventories and the decline or growth in the consumer demand. Hawtrey advocates that credit never be contracted.

Hawtrey's explanation, rooted in Alfred Marshall's writings, is admirable in its simplicity. It contains three elements that are retained in the profit-motive explanation given in chapter 4: variations in the extension of credit, in inventories, and in the consumer demand. These, however, are insufficient in themselves to explain the cycles. Indeed the briskness of economic activity is likely to be affected, though not exclusively, by the volume of credit, but it remains to be explained why the extension of credit varies. The variations are not caused by the fickleness of financiers; they are determined by concrete and definable economic factors. Bankers have good reasons to decline requests for credit when anticipated yields and the risk factor do not warrant a loan. Thus it seems highly questionable whether artificially boosted credit either is sound or can prevent business cycles. Nevertheless, the three elements singled out by Hawtrey as influencing the level of economic activity are probably among the chief offenders and, if in turn explained by underlying forces, could constitute valid elements of a more complete theory.

Evaluation. Ralph Hawtrey's explanation is insufficient because it considers the extension of credit as an independent variable, susceptible of being manipulated at will. The explanation ignores underlying microeconomic phenomena, which may explain why the extension of credit follows a sinusoid rather than a straight line. The same applies to merchants' inventories and the consumer demand. Hawtrey did not investigate the microfoundations of their behavior.

The Overinvestment Theories. These theories describe the overexpansion of capital-goods industries as compared with consumer-goods industries. Capital-goods industries are known to be susceptible to wider cyclical fluctuations than those producing consumer goods. During expansion, capital-goods industries produce facilities exceeding the capacity of the economy to absorb the outputs of these facilities on a permanent basis. This leads to an imbalance in the production process and sooner or later to a crisis. Thus described, the phenomenon explains what happens when cycles are already underway, not what causes the cycles.

Monetary Factors. Three categories of overinvestment theories may be distinguished in accordance with the explanation given of the cause of the overexpansion. The first category includes theories that ascribe the overinvestment to monetary factors. It is represented by such authors as Friedrich A. Hayek, Fritz Machlup, and Ludwig von Mises. Their explanation brings together the reciprocal influence of variations in credit, in interest rates, and in capital investments. Fluctuating credit and interest rates undoubtedly would affect the rate of investments, and overinvestments may well ensue. However, why should credit and interest rates move periodically up or down? These authors have nevertheless identified potent elements of a complete explanation of the cycles that, if supplemented by more fundamental factors, could account for their necessary causation.

Evaluation. The influence of credit and interest rates on investment into the factors of production is a purely macroeconomic explanation of business cycles. That explanation stops short of questioning the forces that influence credit and interest rates at the microeconomic level and might explain why business cycles are inevitable.

Nonmonetary Factors. The second category of overinvestment theories is represented by Arthur A.C. Spiethoff, Gustav Cassel, Knut Wicksell, and Joseph A. Schumpeter. They explain overinvestment through factors other than monetary ones. Spiethoff accounts for overproduction in certain sectors of the economy at the peak of the cycle by a lack of manpower and of consumer goods in other sectors, which causes a rise in interest rates. The revival, say these authors, is due to fresh capital investment. Schumpeter adds that at this moment in the cycle, innovations proliferate; technical advances may have been dormant while times were adverse, but now that the climate is more auspicious, practical applications become profitable. These authors have pointed out the relations between variations in the consumer demand, in interest rates, in the frequency of innovations, and in capital investments. Again, the question is begged: why should the first factor influencing all the others be endowed with a cyclical movement? The theory only pushes the cause a step further back; we still need a basic explanation. The authors nevertheless have singled out variables that play a significant role in the overall chain of causative factors, provided the first cause is included.

Evaluation. The basic explanation must be sought in the microfoundations of macrobehavior. The microfoundations must furnish a good and sufficient reason for inefficiency in the economic process. The authors of this second category have stopped short of bringing to light the underlying economic strains and stresses.

The Acceleration Principle. The third category seeks to explain overinvestment through variations in the consumer demand. Authors who have advanced these theories include Albert Aftalion, Mentor Bouniatian, John M. Clark, Simon S. Kuznets, Arthur C. Pigou, and Roy F. Harrod. Their explanation rests on the observation that minute variations in the consumer demand generate much larger fluctuations in the demand for production facilities. From that tendency has come the concept of the acceleration principle.

Statistical evidence supports the acceleration principle, which applies at all stages of production and distribution. It applies to the construction of production facilities in relation to the manufacture of consumer goods, as also to the output of every stage in relation to the output of subsequent stages.

The acceleration principle has fascinated many economists. Paul A. Samuelson has shown that, coupled with the Keynesian multiplier, the acceleration principle could wreck the economy. Why doesn't it? Could it be that some self-regulating mechanisms in the economy are still operating?

Can the acceleration principle be acknowledged as a valid explanation of business cycles? The answer is simple: if the consumer demand is possessed of cyclical fluctuations, the demand for production facilities mirrors those fluctuations but with increased amplitude. If the consumer demand is stable, there is nothing to amplify. Thus, by explaining business cycles through the acceleration principle, these authors simply relegate the problem one step further, and it is necessary to explain in turn why the consumer demand fluctuates cyclically.

In short, the acceleration principle describes the relationship between two sectors of the economy but does not explain why they both fluctuate. Business-cycle theories abound in explanations of this sort; they fail to reach down deep enough. The authors of the third category of overinvestment theories nonetheless have contributed the description of the disturbances that ensue when consumer demand is subjected to the prime causes of business cycles.

Evaluation. These authors have failed to show why, in a vertically specialized and speculative economy, the consumer demand periodically fluctuates with such wide amplitude, from satiation to voracious appetite, and why most segments of the population manifest the same inclination at the same time. Only the microfoundations of such behavior can answer that question. The profit incentive is the motive power behind it all. When profit margins are distorted, the entire economy is unstable.

Theories Based on Costs, Horizontal Maladjustments, and Indebtedness. Although these theories may be incompletely worked out and awkwardly expressed, some of them contain thoughts that may point in the direction of future discoveries.

Cost Theories. When expected prices no longer cover production costs, say their authors, the profit margin is bound to disappear, and this leads to a curtailment of industrial output. Not only are these findings refreshingly free from monetary concerns, but they focus attention on the mechanism that in the long run affects most profoundly the stability of the economy: the role of the profit margin in regulating production and distribution. The breakdown, these authors go on to say, is due to a disequilibrium between production and consumption, demand having fallen short of supply. This is inadequately explained. Yet chronic, multistage supply-and-demand disparities are very real. They are potent enough to account for economic instability. In turn, instability, with a host of amplifying elements, invites the incidence and periodic iteration of business cycles. The authors of the production-cost theories may thus have started digging in the right field.

Wesley C. Mitchell, the pioneer of business-cycle measurement, pointed out the reinforcing influence of overhead and other fixed costs upon the amplitude of cyclical fluctuations. Total variable costs, which are functions of output volume, increase as the demand rises and fall when the demand slackens. But fixed costs, continuing at a more or less constant level, accentuate rising and falling trends by reducing unit costs during expansion and increasing them during contraction. This may not explain the prime causes of business cycles but serves to show that once an underlying tendency toward economic instability has become energized, it is subject to a variety of amplifying influences. Mitchell was quite aware of the limitations of his finding; in his professional probity, he was not given to overstatements. When *Business Cycles and Their Causes,* the third volume in his series on business cycles was published in 1941, his consent to the use of the word *causes* in the title was given, he confided, only at the insistence of the publisher.

The discrepancy between the cross-market flow of goods and volume of the demand has been noted by John Maynard Keynes and his adepts. They called it the "failure of markets to clear." That designation remained metaphysical because it was never defined or explained in terms of microeconomic realities. It is plain that, on any one market, clearance is always assured. When the buyer is willing to pay one dollar and the seller is willing to accept one dollar, the sale is always consummated. When a price is unacceptable to one or the other party, there is no sale, but neither can it be said that the market failed to clear.

If market clearance refers to fulfillment of sellers' and buyers' expectations in the market or is defined as occurring at a price that leaves no regrets about commitments, then the meaning of that expression is reduced to that of profit maximization. It seems obvious that in a vertical succession of six firms, each of which has eleven competitors, the chances of all seventy-two guesses being consistently accurate are practically nil, so profits are almost never maximized. There exists, indeed, a problem of profit maximization. Nevertheless the failure to maximize profits is inadequate to explain business cycles.

The failure of markets to clear over a period of time occurs only when a succession of markets is involved, when speculative production distorts profit margins, and these convey inaccurate signals to consecutive firms. Despite the somewhat unreal designation and inaccurate definition, that may be precisely what was suspected by Keynes and others using that phrase.

Occasional instances of nonclearing markets may arise even in a nonspeculative economy, but these are quickly dispelled by a price movement. The chronic and cumulative type of nonclearance is linked to a malady of the profit motive. Because it never shows up on the surface, each individual market tending to clear all of the time, the concept remains a mystery.

Evaluation. The authors of business-cycle theories based on costs have delved into microconcepts such as prices, costs, and profits. They have pointed to disequilibria between production and consumption, implying a vertical succession of markets because on each market supply and demand tend to be equated. They do not attempt further explanation of how multistage disequilibria can subsist chronically in the face of promptly clearing individual markets. Among other investigations, a thorough analysis of the price mechanism and its links to the determination of profit margins remains to be undertaken.

Maladjustment Theories. A number of authors believe that horizontal maladjustments generate business cycles. They claim that horizontal maladjustments (disproportions between parallel industries) are organically related to vertical disequilibria (disproportions between subordinated industries). These concepts could become relevant if accurately expressed. Among those who have advanced them are Frank W. Taussig, Arthur C. Pigou, Thomas W. Mitchell, and Sir William H. Beveridge.

Horizontal and vertical maladjustments are in need of definition. Since individual markets always clear, no maladjustments can be detected on any one market for very long. Vertical maladjustments involve more than one market, but these authors use *maladjustments* to refer exclusively to an improperly proportioned emphasis given to producers' goods and facilities versus consumer goods. The overinvestment theories, regardless of their category, had already brought out that relationship, which explains only what happens after the cycles are already underway. The profit-motive theory of business cycles is concerned with imbalances in the incentives allocated to successive stages in the production and distribution of consumer goods. Although such imbalances can also be described as vertical maladjustments, both the nature and causes of the latter are essentially different. We may face here a problem of semantics.

In the literature, the term *disequilibrium* seems to be used interchangeably with *maladjustment*. As applied to a single market, disequilibrium can only be temporary. Economists have been pointlessly debating whether the Keynesian model is one of equilibrium or disequilibrium. Markets should be viewed as mobiles. At every moment in time, the mobile strikes a posture of equilibrium, which is the result of all of the physical forces exerted on it up to that moment. Every market always tends toward equilibrium, the result of all the economic forces exerted on it up to the present.

On any one market, disequilibrium can be the result only of limited elasticity in demand and/or supply, or of slow responses. However, in vertical marketing channels, speculative production results in chronic disequilibria; these are the rule rather than the exception. The distinction between individual markets and the pipeline is essential in explaining disequilibria. The same remarks apply to maladjustments.

Those authors who have raised some suspicions about adjustments and equilibria have shown unerring intuition and paved the way for further progress in the study of multimarket phenomena. When interstage relations are analyzed, especially from the standpoint of the vertical allocation of profit margins, it becomes clear that vertical maladjustments are inevitable. These necessarily generate inefficiencies in the fulfillment of the consumer demand. For that reason, the vertical maladjustment theories deserve commendation.

Evaluation. The authors of the horizontal and vertical maladjustment theories of business cycles, however, have not shown within the framework of microeconomics why entrepreneurs attempting to maximize profits invariably end up generating maladjustments. That conflict remains to be substantiated and explained. It can be understood only when a vertical succession of markets, and speculative production and distribution, are incorporated into the model and the dynamics of prices and profits are exhaustively analyzed. As Walras assumed, price changes must be freely transferable between markets. In a specialized and speculative model, they cannot be.

Indebtedness Theory. Indebtedness impressed Irving Fisher with its violent consequences at the first signs of a downturn in the cycle. Overcommitted borrowers—home owners, stockholders on margin, commodity traders, industrial debtors, or simply installment buyers—may find themselves embarrassed should they lose their employment or other source of revenue. Foreclosures, liquidations, and repossessions may then cascade upon them, precipitating a chain reaction. This describes what took place during the depression of the 1930s, as seen by Fisher. It does not explain why a downturn occurred in 1929. However, Fisher provides an eloquent account of how the crisis, once triggered, propagates in a rush from one sector of the economy to another.

Evaluation. Although Irving Fisher is concerned with credit and debt, he describes only their results once the cycle has passed its peak; he does not explain ups and downs in the extension of credit and is subject to the same critique as is Hawtrey who based his business-cycle theory on credit alone. Both ignore the forces that make the extension of credit fluctuate.

Underconsumption Theories. Advanced by such authors as John A. Hobson, William T. Foster, Waddill Catchings, and Emil Lederer, these theories appear incomplete, unconvincing, and difficult to condense. The starting point is a growing economy, which gives an impetus to producers. The purchasing power of the population may then be insufficient to absorb the entire output; also an insufficient money supply may slow transactions. The result takes on the aspect of underconsumption.

The lack of purchasing power is what needs to be explained. Say's Law maintained that it could not occur. If it does, there must be a substantial reason for it. As for the money supply, the monetary theory has already covered it. Thus, the argument in the underconsumption theories is partly inadequate to explain the tendency and partly preempted by other theories. The same can be said of theories based on excessive savings and on insufficient wage increases.

Who says underconsumption says overproduction. We have never yet had general overproduction, only underproduction at inflated prices, leading to a waste in purchasing power. That would result in apparent underconsumption. Frustrated consumers are reluctant to acquire goods at prices out of line with their economic value. The authors sensed a problem, described it awkwardly, and satisfied themselves with an incomplete explanation. To be resolved, the problem must first be stated solidly and in accurate terms susceptible of mathematical expression. Then an explanation must be given capable of accounting for the problem. That the authors of the underconsumption theories have failed to achieve, but they should be given credit for questioning certain economic relationships that, when more fully developed, can throw light on the business cycle problem.

Evaluation. The underconsumption theories lack an investigation of microfoundations of the macroconcepts their authors advance in the hope of explaining cycles. Why are purchasing power and the money supply, the rate of savings and wage demands endowed with gyrating motions? What is it that the entrepreneur does that has such untoward effects? Unless such questions are answered, cycles remain an unsolved mystery.

Psychological Theories. The psychological factor has been invoked by a number of authors who have not been able to explain cycles through purely economic factors. Even Keynes sought refuge in that metaphysical realm. The truth of the matter is that an incursion into the field of psychology is both illusory and unnecessary. The field of psychology is foreign to basic economic problems and cannot help in either stating or solving them. Moreover, the answers are waiting to be found in the economic pipeline by anyone curious enough to investigate it.

Some of the psychological theories simply go astray. The challenge is to find out why, for a given consumer demand, the natural pursuit of maximum profits by producers and financiers causes business cycles. The problem is an unresolved economic problem. In other theories, the term *psychological* is a misnomer. They have already been examined under other designations. The consequences of false predictions concerning prices and quantities have already been discussed by the authors of the horizontal maladjustment theory. Note that business expectations are not accounted for by subjective fickleness of entrepreneurs but by objective economic factors. Among the factors are such hazards as market uncertainty and uncertainty of income. Nevertheless, the psychological theories divulge at least a deep-seated dissatisfaction and impatience with existing explanations; they seek a totally fresh approach toward the conquest of the plague of business cycles. It is necessary to recognize the superficiality of past constructs before attempting to undergird them with a sound and solid foundation.

Evaluation. The psychological theories have failed to accomplish a thorough investigation of the dynamics of the profit motive. But none of the techniques developed to date by psychologists can be of help in studying how profit margins are determined, how they are linked to the vertical cross-market operation of the price mechanism, or how they can become distorted. The problem is purely economic.

In conclusion, among the large number of authors, comprising geniuses and great thinkers, who have wrestled with business cycles, few have looked beyond proximate causes. Those few have here been flagged and praised. They have lighted a path that may be followed toward basic progress and have shown that no revolution is necessary—just continued evolution of familiar mainstream economic thought.

The Keynesian Theory of Unemployment

John Maynard Keynes considered that his advances in unemployment theory provided a sufficient and satisfying explanation of business cycles. Few economists today would uphold such a view. How could a strictly static theory account for an essentially dynamic phenomenon? Furthermore, like most other business-cycle theories, the Keynesian system is macroeconomic in character; it fails to identify the microfoundations of bewildering nationwide phenomena. If basic progress is to be made, it will be necessary to descend not only to the microlevel of the individual firm but to the sublevel of isolated transactions executed by that firm on particular markets and involving specific units of given products.

The Keynesian model is a considerably more realistic description of the economy, in which periodic fluctuations in prices, wages, and output are facts of life. Keynes broke away from the classics and neoclassics who denied or ignored the possibility of business cycles. Unfortunately a realistic acknowledgment of the existence of cyclical fluctuations neither explains the cause of nor provides the cure for that obstinate peril. What is needed is not merely a more accurate description of reality or a look into the microeconomy but an analysis of those features of a speculative multistage economy that relate to the free vertical transfer of price changes between markets. That was far removed from the minds of Keynes and his followers.

Although the Keynesian model lacks a number of characteristics required of a valid business-cycle theory, it nevertheless lends itself to conversion into such a theory. It needs the infrastructure provided by a system of thought describing the dynamics of prices and profits in a speculative multistage economy. Such a system of thought may explain why the "independent variables" of the Keynesian model behave as they do, thus providing the missing underpinnings that Keynes himself had given up hope of grasping.

The Keynesian paradigm lays a more valid claim as a theory of unemployment. The level of employment in that paradigm is determined at each moment in time by four variables: liquidity preference and the money supply (which together govern the rate of interest), the marginal efficiency of capital (which with the first two variables limits the size of investments), and the marginal propensity to consume (complement of the reciprocal of the multiplier). That formula for determining the level of employment does not seem to have been disputed. Its chief weakness lies in the fact that Keynes accepted the four factors as "independent variables" and made no effort to dig for their microfoundations. They are not independent. They depend on economic, not psychological, factors of high potency. In the profit-motive theory, such economic factors exist in the form of profit margins. When profit margins are distorted, as they seem to be in a modern, industrial economy, they tend to influence the variables of the Keynesian model in a way that explains a great deal of inefficiency and waste. Profit-margin distortions, through their interface with the Keynesian variables, are capable of curtailing employment. The two theories together present an explanation of the roots of unemployment.

By itself, the Keynesian unemployment theory is incomplete. Why should investors prefer liquidity? Why should the money supply become insufficient? Why should the efficiency of capital become eroded? Why should workers choose to curtail their consumption? These are legitimate questions that Keynes was not prepared to answer. It is manifest that for all its prestige, the Keynesian theory never explained why unemployment exists in an industrial economy. Yet a valid explanation is a condition of success in developing a preventive program; without it, the hope of avoiding unemployment on a permanent basis is scant indeed.

Evaluation. The lengthy Keynesian interlude represents a step forward in establishing macroeconomic relationships, but it is in need of reinforcement through the addition of dynamic microeconomic foundations in order that unemployment might be more fully explained and prevented.

Post Keynesian Economic Theory

After the vivid interest in unemployment and business cycles during the first forty years of this century, the concern for economic prosperity and stability has waned. Monetary policy whipped the demand; if necessary, more fuel could be added. Recessions took on the mild form of decreases in the rate of growth, until the advent of stagflation. We are now again plagued by unemployment and business cycles. Keynes was helpful during the period when little help was needed. Now Keynes is forgotten.

Among the names associated most often with the Post Keynesian school are Kenneth J. Arrow, Paul Davidson, John K. Galbraith, Frank H. Hahn, John R. Hicks, Nicholas L. Kaldor, Joan Robinson, Piero Sraffa, and Sidney Weintraub. Rather than investigating unemployment and business cycles, these authors reverted to the favorite but less relevant themes of the past: equilibrium, market clearance, the passage of time, economic uncertainty, expectations, money and credit, interest rates, savings, the multiplier and the acceleration principle, economic models, and realism.

Paul Davidson summarizes the objectives of the Post Keynesian school under three captions.

1. *The economy is a process in historical time.* In my view, this is a healthy reaction against static theories of the past. Indeed what is required is a dynamic model that provides for the passage of time and permits the observation and control of self-adjusting mechanisms.

2. *In a world where uncertainty and surprises are unavoidable, expectations have a necessary and significant effect on economic outcomes.* That thinking prompts the following comments: Market uncertainty, a man-made malady, can be eliminated by avoiding speculative production. If this at first appears to be an abstraction, there may be more than one way of removing market uncertainty, and if so it no longer needs to be considered unavoidable. As for expectations and their effects, these too can perhaps be reduced to manageable proportions. More importantly, except for minor and local instability, such as the cobweb phenomenon, unemployment and business cycles probably can never be fully explained by as weak a cause as the feedback of expectations, correct or erroneous. Modern economic ills would most likely continue essentially as before, even if all expectations were always correct and profits maximized.

3. *Political and economic institutions are not negligible; in fact, they play an extremely important role in determining real-world economic outcomes.* I disagree. Contrary to the warnings of classical economists, Keynes, who accepted unemployment as unavoidable, placed his trust in the government for its control. If it should become possible to conquer unemployment through the application of improved business-management techniques, political institutions would play a diminishing role in determining economic outcomes. As the focus is switched to the pursuit of greater efficiency in meeting the consumer demand as a means of conquering unemployment and business cycles, economic institutions may likewise lose their importance.

Another topic of particular interest to the Post Keynesian school is the importance of money. Adherents believe that modern monetary economies do not possess an automatic mechanism that ensures a tendency toward full employment of resources over time. I believe that a multistage study of the price mechanism may reveal whether it operates efficiently, and if not, why not. Once we know why it does not operate efficiently, we can take measures to remove possible impediments and see that it performs freely. The purpose of this book is to show that every modern economy possesses such an automatic mechanism that can ensure a tendency toward full employment of resources over time. Post Keynesian economists also believe that underemployment equilibrium is a recurring phenomenon in money-using production economies. But they may have misstated the problem. Perhaps it should be formulated in these terms: underemployment equilibrium is a recurring phenomenon in multistage economies characterized by speculative production and distribution. The prime causes of underemployment may be quite independent of money. Finally, Post Keynesian economists believe that the existence of underemployment equilibrium must be associated with the characteristics of money and related institutions and with how production is organized. Again the problem may be inaccurately worded. Instead of being associated with money and related institutions, underemployment equilibrium, one of the two components of stagflation, may be the penalty of speculative production in a multistage economy.

Evaluation. To summarize, the Post Keynesian school of economic thinking has broken away from its forty-year subservience to the tenets of the great British economist. It has branched out to include a broad selection of topics that may have some impact on the utilization of resources. It is a natural reaction to frustrations experienced from Keynesianism when it ran into stagflation. There is, among the themes pursued by the Post Keynesians, little that is new. Their thinking gets trapped into the lure of expectations and the bait of money when real solutions may only be found at the antipodes. What the Post Keynesian school is not doing is to investigate microfoundations of the economic process, in particular the dynamics of self-adjusting mechanisms.

Mainstream of Economic Theory Today

Relevant Characteristics

In a modest cooperative book titled *The Crisis in Economic Theory,* edited by
Daniel Bell and Irving Kristol, Paul Davidson qualifies the corpus of orthodox
neoclassical theory as a shambles. The disarray is great, says another publication. Never have there been so many economists in possession of the most
advanced tools and techniques, and never have they come up with such con-
tradictory theories or recommendations.

There is hardly a single mainstream of economic thinking today. There
are neoclassicists, Post Keynesians, and Marxists; monetarists, the Austrian
school, and institutionalists; and many others.

A number of authors have expressed prophetic views of what may be the
next step forward in economic theory. As seen from the standpoint of a group
of dissidents (the Union for Radical Political Economy, organized at the University of Michigan in 1968), the group of prominent economists who constitute the elite of the American Economic Association hide their ideology under
the cloak of mathematics and internal logic, but their hypotheses are weak
and unrealistic, their scope is limited. They neglect the most important social
problems (such as inequality of incomes and externalities) or dismiss socio-
economic conflicts (unemployment, business cycles) as *a dysfunction of
adjustment mechanisms.* If this is an accurate appraisal of their thinking, then
this elite is truly heralding the next important step forward: the thorough
study of adjustment mechanisms and their dysfunctions. That is the task of
this book. Such an investigation can correct far-reaching social and even ethical inadequacies inherited from the past.

In the same vein and typical of innumerable such statements throughout
the economic literature, Robert Clower and Axel Leijonhufvud have argued
that Keynes's *General Theory* discusses disequilibria or the breakdown of a
variety of adjustment mechanisms. Their interpretation again points to a
potentially highly productive development of economic theory: what are the
functions of the price mechanism, why does it not function efficiently, and
what means can be designed to correct the deficiency? If these three questions
can be answered, basic progress may be achieved.

More evidence of forward thinking came out of a conference sponsored
in 1969 by the Committee on Economic Stability of the Social Science Research Council. The conference entitled "Is the Business Cycle Obsolete?"
concluded that since business cycles are still with us, the severe depression in
the research on business cycles ought to be terminated.

One of the most forward looking economists and explicit critics of this
generation is Janos Kornai. Kornai has no patience with the Walrasian single-
stage model in which intermarket conflicts are disregarded and which does

not lend itself to the study of multistage control phenomena. What needs to be studied, according to Kornai, is the multimarket dynamics of the price mechanism.

Other signs of what the future may hold for researchers are to be found in discussions of markets. Market imperfections and market failures are an observation frequently recorded in the literature, but there has not been a comprehensive theory of market structures. Now, following the lead given fifty years ago by Edward H. Chamberlin, who developed a theory of distinct product markets, William Nordhaus and Arthur Okun discriminate between "auction" markets and "administered" markets—what Sir John Hicks calls "flexprice" markets and "fixprice" markets. The distinction represents the first step in developing a list of impediments to the efficient relay of price fluctuations between vertically aligned markets. Price setting on administered or fixprice markets obviously retards such relay.

Friedrich A. Hayek has great faith in the price mechanism as a highly effective, decentralized, and unconscious system that far exceeds what the human mind could contrive. Its real function is to communicate information, a function that Hayek concedes is fulfilled less perfectly as prices grow more rigid. Price rigidities, which Hayek left unexplained, are another impediment to the relay of price fluctuations between successive markets in vertical channels.

With intuition and clarity, Peter F. Drucker has set down the specifications for the next step forward in economic theory. It must transcend Keynes. It will again be microeconomics, although it must accomplish what Marshall failed to do: integrate microeconomics and macroeconomics. It will be centered on supply and productivity. We do not now possess a model embracing these. The new economics will attack basic assumptions of existing theory, the paradigm, not just this or that theory. It may start with productivity or capital formation. Productivity may be used as a basis for a new theory of value. The new economics will be humanity, moral philosophy, and science.

Although Drucker's description of the new economics sounds like a total break with past trends of thought, in reality it is only an extension of earlier concepts through the inclusion of neglected areas and elements. Without the hypothesis of the consequences of speculative production, it would have been very difficult to identify what had been neglected that is relevant. With it, the identification became unmistakable.

The primary purpose of economic activity is the efficient satisfaction of consumer wants. Much evidence suggests that for all his legendary know-how, the American entrepreneur may not yet have learned how to accomplish this. It is for the economist to teach him how. Certain physical incompatibilities may be found to stand in the way of efficient production and distribution. The business profession has not yet detected their hidden source. Stagflation research should address the problem of the efficient satisfaction of consumer wants if it hopes to make a permanent contribution to the prevention of stagflation.

Some of the thinking of leading exponents of mainstream economics may end up not being fruitful. The emphasis on macroeconomic phenomena to the exclusion of their microfoundations has generated much misdirected effort. The obsession with money has led economists astray and the American economy to the brink of disaster. The money hypnosis goes back to the Industrial Revolution, when unemployment and business cycles became a problem. What changes took place at that time? Economists suspected the use of money for investment in production facilities and equipment. Money has explained and can explain very little. Theorists remained unaware of other changes that occurred at the same time and for the same reasons. These concern vertical specialization and speculative production.

Say's Law that the supply creates its own demand is still believed by many economists to apply in a barter economy. This would imply that it may not be applicable in a money and credit economy. That concept may be in error. Say's Law may be fully valid, regardless of money and credit, in a nonspeculative economy; it may be inapplicable in real life in a multistage economy characterized by speculative production and may have been obsolete for 150 years.

The overwhelming concern with public policy may be an admission of defeat. The economy is not behaving correctly, so the government is pressured into straightening it out. This is a premature capitulation. Other options may be more promising. Why not instead channel thought and energy into researching and resolving the problem of the economy's less-than-efficient stance?

The building block, in the Walrasian model, is the agent. It has led to a static, telescoped economic system. A better building block, or economic atom, may be the transaction because it suggests movement, flow. The economic molecule might then be the vertical chain of transactions, from the sale of raw materials to the purchase of consumer goods. It is realistic; it suggests a dynamic, multistage algorithm suitable for describing a speculative production economy.

One day Albert Einstein was talking with a group of economists about scientific methodology. His advice to them was a surprise. They would not make real headway, he told them, so long as they continued making only empirical observations. They should make hypotheses and then verify them. The profit-motive theory of unemployment and business cycles emanated from a hypothesis I first advanced in 1939.

To be specific, a normal, healthy, efficient economy may be hypothesized by reference to which our subnormal, ailing, inefficient economy can be explained. The hypothesis may provide a bridge from the real to the hypothetical economy. The hypothetical economy would then become a generalized model, of which the real economy would be one special case. The profit-motive theory was born of such thinking. Someday it may be recognized as a generalized theory of unemployment and business cycles.

Assumptions Subject to Reappraisal

Listed next are a series of assumptions generally shared by economists of varied persuasions, which may have been responsible for holding back progress and should now be questioned and reexamined.

1. One of the most unfortunate assumptions, because it delayed progress in the development of economic theory, is that a vertical sequence of markets is but a replication of a single market and that it is a safe simplification to telescope them into one market—a single market may present no problem; problems are more likely to reside in the pipeline.

2. The second most regrettable assumption may have been that a vertical sequence of markets, each of which is separately efficient, is also efficient—equilibrium may exist on each market within the vertical channel, and yet chronic disequilibrium reign between successive markets.

These first two assumptions were made by Leon Walras when he assumed that price changes are freely transferable between markets. That may be the Achilles' heel of contemporary thought about stagflation.

3. For the above reasons, the famous Arrow-Debreu models, previously assumed to be true representations of the economy, may be unrealistic and may have to be expanded to include a vertical succession of markets.

4. The price mechanism has been assumed to operate dependably and to bring about the desirable adjustments—this may be true on an individual market but cannot be depended on in a speculative, multistage economy.

5. Profit margins have been assumed to be dependable signals for entrepreneurs to maximize for greatest efficiency—this may not be possible unless the price mechanism is permitted to operate dependably.

6. It has been assumed with Adam Smith that under free competition, the market price gravitates toward the natural price—that concept applies to a nonspeculative economy; it may be incompatible with speculative production and may have been obsolete for over 150 years.

7. It has been assumed that under free competition, in accordance with Adam Smith's concept of the invisible hand, the maximization of profit by selfish entrepreneurs is to the best advantage of society—that concept applies to a nonspeculative economy and may long have been obsolete.

8. It has been assumed that any disparity between intent and result in the conduct of business flows from an error of knowledge—information is not the equivalent of the profit incentive. Where they clash (and they frequently do because they do not travel through the same channels), the incentive gov-

erns. *Unemployment and business cycles may be due not to a lack of information but to faulty incentives.*

9. Market uncertainty, pertaining to the consumer demand at an array of prices, has been assumed unavoidable—it would be eliminated in a nonspeculative economy and may be considerably reduced in a speculative economy through the application of appropriate management techniques.

10. Expectations with regard to demand versus costs have been assumed to have a decisive bearing on the behavior of the economy—there may be much more potent economic forces at work (profit incentives) in determining economic behavior so that expectations may end up playing but a minor role. Besides, expectations are rendered unnecessary in a nonspeculative economy and can also be reduced in importance in real life. Unless there is an underlying tendency toward instability, erroneous expectations cancel one another.

11. It has been assumed that suboptimum behavior of the economy can be corrected through growth—the objective function of the von Neumann and various turnpike models has been maximization of the rate of growth. Growth has been a fetish. If the economy is understood and its efficiency increased, it will not need growth to cover up deficiencies; neither will natural growth depend on extraneous stimulation.

12. It has been assumed that markets may not clear for protracted periods—that is a metaphysical concept never properly defined. Subject to limitations in the elasticity of demand and supply, every individual market always clears. Nonclearance applies to a vertical succession of markets and covers a real phenomenon that needs explicit specification. It is not confined to erroneous expectations or failure to maximize profits.

13. Pareto-optimality has been defined as existing when no one can be made better off without making one or more other parties worse off. It has been assumed that when Pareto-optimality has been attained in a speculative economy, this is actually the maximum satisfaction that can accrue to all agents involved—in reality, the aggregate satisfaction is subject to being further increased through the application of management methods equivalent to nonspeculative production. This would result in a new optimality at a higher level. Another way of expressing the same thought is that speculative production necessarily creates an economic entropy or lack of efficiency that is not present in a nonspeculative economy.

14. It has been assumed that since economic behavior has not been fully explained through economic factors, it will be necessary to invade the territory of psychology to find the "ultimate independent variables" and resolve the issue—This may be an admission of failure. Highly potent economic factors exist that can account for economic inefficiency.

15. It has been assumed that because it deals with the human element, which may not act rationally and may change its mind, economics can uncover no constants or regularities and does not lend itself to dependable predictions

—that may be because economic theory, so far applicable only in an unrealistic nonspeculative economy, has not yet advanced to the status of explaining a real, speculative economy. When that occurs, regularities and constants may emerge, basic and necessary cause-and-effect relationships may be revealed, and new theorems may be formulated. Predictions based on these may be reliable. Economics may take on some of the attributes of the physical sciences.

16. Fluctuating inventory levels have been assumed to generate cyclical fluctuations—inventories are but buffers between consecutive markets; they reflect intermarket suctions or pressures due to the inefficient relay of price fluctuations and resulting profit-margin distortions.

Certain studies have ascribed inventory cycles to producers' erroneous expectations. What is not explained in those studies is why a majority of producers should for months on end make optimistic predictions, leading to growing inventories or why at other times a majority should make pessimistic decisions for many weeks, resulting in shrinking inventories. Erroneous expectations no doubt are widespread, but they would normally be random and cancel one another. Only preexisting cyclical fluctuations affecting the demand could have a general tendency to influence inventory levels one way or the other.

Inventories have fascinated theorists because they are visible and measurable. In reality, they are the tip of the iceberg of underlying tensions that are not apparent on the surface. They are due to chronically conflicting supply-and-demand velocities, defined in terms of the economic value of goods. Such conflicts result from enduring distortions in profit margins. Inventory cycles do not generate, only amplify, business cycles previously triggered by a malady of the profit motive.

2

Premises for the Next Step Forward in Economic Theory

General Objectives

1. The first objective of any new unemployment and business-cycle theory should be proper focus on the main purpose of economic activity: the efficient fulfillment of consumer wants. As long as we do not know how to serve the consumer efficiently, meaning at lowest cost, stagflation may remain unavoidable.

2. The building blocks for a new theory should be appropriate to depicting a dynamic and vibrant activity endowed with constant movement and flow. It is proposed that the individual transaction be selected for the economic atom. Note that there may be no inefficiency in the individual transaction. The economic molecule, or aggregate of atoms, would then be the vertical chain of transactions linking the raw-material producer to the ultimate consumer. The entire problem of stagflation may reside within the economic molecule, the pulsating activity that travels through the pipeline. Thus it is well to discriminate between the sound economic atom and the ailing economic molecule.

3. The third objective should be realism in designing mathematical models of the economy. A large number of factors have been proposed to make economic models conform more closely to reality. Many factors are more or less irrelevant. They consist of refining existing models with detail that contributes little of consequence and unnecessarily clutters the system of equations. It is important to add only refinements essential to the theory.

One cardinal refinement is the inclusion into mathematical models of the economic pipeline, made up of stages and markets along vertical marketing channels. The pipeline is the passage through which the chain of transactions links the first producer to the last user. The pipeline has always been known to exist; however, no one suspected that it might add a dimension of depth to economic theory. If progress is to be made, it is indispensable to explore the pipeline in its entire length, from mines and fields to consumers. The telescoping of successive markets into a single commodity exchange is a simplification that cannot be consented without emasculating economic theory.

Realistic models can be designed through the inclusion of sequential stages and markets. These will provide a laboratory where multistage control phenomena and self-adjusting mechanisms will come into view and can be investigated. Although each successive market may be in equilibrium, intermarket disequilibrium may be revealed. The Arrow-Debreu models may have

27

limited realism or applicability until they include a sequence of stages and markets.

4. With the inclusion of the hitherto missing dimension into economic models, it now becomes possible to hypothesize a broader, fully efficient economy of which the current limping reality is but a special case. The hypothesis permits escaping from the shackles of the current improperly operating economy. The more that economy is observed empirically, the more the student may become hypnotized by it. Instead he can break away from that which is imperfect and grasp what is safe, sound, and efficient. The broader economy need not be represented in the world today; if it can be defined mathematically, its imaginary, abstract nature will not matter. It will provide the bridge that links the present reality to a better economy. That broader concept may be a hypothetical, nonspeculative economy. And the theory that relates to it may be a generalized theory of efficiency, full employment, and stability.

5. A theory can be developed that integrates microeconomics and macroeconomics, by providing the microfoundations of macroeconomic behavior.

6. Few immutable relationships have been discovered in the field of economics. Everything seems to change with time. A search for immutable relationships may now become possible, including the most useful type of such relationships: authentic necessary cause-and-effect relationships. Their discovery may help chart a normative course.

7. Among the economy's self-regulating mechanisms is the price mechanism. It has long been conceded that it does not function with full efficiency. An important objective of any new stagflation theory is the study in depth, or multistage study, of the price mechanism, the requisites for its effective operation, the impediments it may encounter, and the measures that may be required to remove the impediments.

8. The most potent force known in economics is the profit motive. Should anything go wrong with it, we should expect both confusion and waste. Profit margins must be investigated in depth. It must be determined what are the prerequisites for their proper interstage equilibration, their relationship with the operation of the price mechanism, and the precautions that are indicated to prevent interstage imbalances. In the past, the emphasis has been on prompt and accurate communication of information, to the exclusion of measures aimed at accurately balanced profit margins at successive stages. Only the latter have a bearing on stagflation. The impact of profit-margin distortions on macrobehavior of the economy is so pronounced that the theory presented here has been designated the profit-motive theory of unemployment and business cycles.

9. A new stagflation theory should also determine why Adam Smith's basic pronouncements and Say's Law have been impaired for so many generations. Among these are Smith's assertion that under free competition, market prices gravitate toward natural prices and that profit maximization, as

though under the influence of an invisible hand, benefits society; and Say's postulate that supply creates its own demand. The new theory should then show the way toward a full reinstatement of all three contentions.

10. The new stagflation theory should include the formulation of a new theory of economic value, essential to the measurement of the cross-market supply-and-demand relationship, as well as to the measurement of the degree of cross-market competitive pressure.

Specific Objectives

No theory has much human value unless it is applicable in real life. The modifications in emphasis suggested for the development of new economic theory are not irrelevant to the resolution of practical problems. On the contrary, it is for the sake of a better understanding of unresolved economic difficulties that general objectives were formulated. Among the specific objectives here contemplated is the control of previously unexplained economic phenomena, all related to the predicament of stagflation.

Market Uncertainty

Frank H. Knight has established the distinction between risk and uncertainty. Risk, he asserts, is an element of cost since it can be avoided through payment of an insurance premium. Economic uncertainty does not possess sufficient regularity in its occurrence to permit elimination; the premium would have to be prohibitive. It gives rise, instead, says Knight, to the entrepreneurial profit.

There exist five distinct categories of economic uncertainty. Proceeding from the exogenous toward the endogenous varieties, the analyst encounters, first, the uncertainty due to meteorological phenomena, such as floods and droughts, and the ensuing irregularity of crops. It can be designated *meteorological uncertainty*. It is practically inevitable and yet much less to be feared than the remaining four. If the latter can be conquered, crop irregularities could be compensated for in large measure through reserves and substitutions. Not that this is not attempted today, but the same measures would become considerably more effective.

Political uncertainty is the second category. Business is made uncertain by changes of administration, tax and tariff revisions, monetary measures, government regulation, and intervention of every description; business is seriously disturbed by strikes, revolution, and war. While political uncertainty is more to be feared than the meteorological type, some of its elements are influenced to an appreciable degree by other factors of uncertainty that may be easier to control—particularly those in the fifth category.

Exogenous economic elements, extraneous to the inner workings of the economy, delineate the third category of uncertainty, called *exogenous economic uncertainty*. Business activities are made uncertain by variations in the extraction of gold and silver, in copper mining, oil production, the discovery or exhaustion of other natural resources, inventions, technological advances, and development of new materials and engineering processes, all of which affect costs—and changes in needs, tastes, and styles, which influence the demand. These are the external shocks that continually rock the economy, dictating constant watchfulness and alert adaptability. It should not be concluded that exogenous impacts are sufficient, in either quality or intensity, to explain stagflation or any of its components. One shock counteracts another, and in time they all die out. Eventually stability tends to return. However, exogenous changes are much more difficult to accommodate when continual endogenous uncertainty is superimposed. The latter may be easier to dislodge, which should, in turn, relieve the pressure of exogenous economic uncertainty.

Expectation uncertainty forms the fourth category. It is caused by insufficient information, long enough in advance, of the product mix and volume that the entrepreneur must supply in order to maximize his profit. Errors of judgment in predicting the future demand in terms of costs not only cut into profits but disappoint consumers. Such errors are, however, incapable of explaining the origin of unemployment and business cycles. Even if erroneous predictions could be completely eliminated, economic stagnation and instability would most likely continue essentially as before. The latter are intimately related to the fifth category of uncertainty. While expectation uncertainty cannot be eliminated, it can be reduced as an extra benefit of bringing under control the uncertainty of the fifty category.

The fifth category of economic uncertainty, *market uncertainty,* is another endogenous factor. It comprises the uncertainty about demand, costs, price movements, and changing economic activity on various markets, unaccountable by identifiable causes. This is by far the most pernicious element. Market uncertainty persists even when all markets are in equilibrium and all profits are maximized. It cannot be eliminated through increased market intelligence or through advances in the art of forecasting cost, demand, or supply. It affects producers, consumers, and financiers alike. Workers and investors are particularly sensitive to the uncertainty of income, a direct by-product of market uncertainty.

Economic uncertainty of the first four categories is intensified by market uncertainty, which complicates the maximization of profits and other phases of business management. It also introduces great hazards into fixed capital investments in industry and commerce. It even influences adversely many political decisions. Market uncertainty should be specifically addressed as one of the problems in need of explanation and control.

Inadequate Purchasing Power and Sales Resistance

Insufficient purchasing power is a problem that Jean-Baptiste Say did not recognize because he wrote before mass unemployment and business cycles appeared in the wake of the Industrial Revolution. His faith that supply creates its own demand reflects the Golden Age—not ours.

In an industrial economy, a gap keeps aggregate supply apart from aggregate demand, at prices equaling the economic value of goods. It is an invisible gap—it cannot be measured—and an irretrievable gap, for the following reasons.

That slice of additional consumer purchasing power that would be required to put to use the nation's idle production capacity is peculiar in that it apparently cannot be created. The government has consistently transferred excess purchasing power from the rich to the poor, and when this is done in moderation out of a balanced budget, probably has no harmful effects. But when the government has recourse to deficit financing to push the demand, it literally robs purchasing power from the taxpayers' children. Such a policy rests on an unfortunate miscalculation, as it dares to consume now a scarce commodity that will be in short supply in future years.

If, then, purchasing power cannot be created, how can it be increased? Purchasing power can be wasted, and the only way to augment its aggregate volume, to coincide with the nation's production capacity, is to stop wasting it. In the present state of development of economic theory, neither the university professor nor the practical entrepreneur knows how the purchasing power of the nation's consumers (or the purchasing power of the currency) can be wasted. The proper approach for recovering the waste is thus a fortiori unknown to them.

One regrettable consequence of the waste of purchasing power is that it depresses the demand in three ways. When some of the potential purchasing power of the nation goes to waste, the effective demand is first limited to the residual purchasing power. But every waste of purchasing power is automatically accompanied by an increase in unit costs of the goods offered for sale. The unit of merchandise with a marginal subjective value below the selling price is then reached well before the last unit is sold. Buyers resist paying inflated prices. The demand is again reduced. Moreover, consumers are sensitive to market uncertainty, which to them means uncertainty of income. They are induced to set aside larger reserves than would normally be required. A third reduction in the demand widens the gap Say's Law had not anticipated.

The last two factors, which together generate aggregate sales resistance, may be coextensive with the desire to lay aside a portion of income for future consumption. Consumers are conscious of only that desire. Should the savings objective exceed the level of combined sales resistance with some individuals, the excess may very likely be offset by the rate of dissaving on the part of others.

All three factors cumulate to limit the effective demand to levels below the productive capacity of the nation. The triple limitation acts as a damper on production and, with wage rigidities what they are, eventually results in mass dismissals of workers. The nation's economic life is threatened.

Figure 2-1 illustrates the relationship of these several concepts; it shows how a waste of potential purchasing power may end up reducing the demand well below the remaining purchasing power. If the original waste of purchasing power could be recovered, sales resistance would automatically disappear, and the available purchasing power may then, in accordance with Say's Law, equal the production capacity of the nation.

The compound problem and its control deserve close attention.

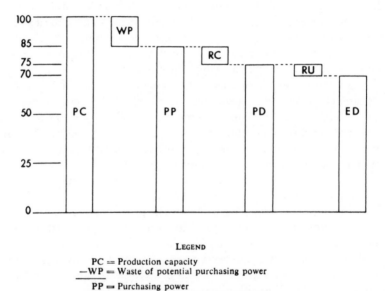

LEGEND

PC = Production capacity
—WP = Waste of potential purchasing power

PP = Purchasing power
—RC = Sales resistance due to excessive costs

PD = Potential demand
—RU = Sales resistance due to uncertainty of income

ED = Effective demand

Figure 2-1. Diagram Showing the Relationship between the Nation's Production Capacity, its Purchasing Power, the Potential, and the Effective Consumer Demand

Note: The economic entropy equals the production capacity minus the effective demand.

Measurement of the Cross-Market
Supply-and-Demand Relationship

The cross-market supply-and-demand relationship has never been measured. On each individual market, there is no occasion to measure it because, as the market price gravitates toward the natural price, so the supply-and-demand relationship gravitates toward equality or equilibrium. That, however, is a single-market assessment of supply and demand.

When all vertically linked markets are taken into account and an in-depth, cross-market supply-and-demand relationship is considered, there is no method known to measure it. The in-depth relationship is that which counts when dealing with the problems of unemployment and business cycles, or stagflation. Not only has the cross-market relationship not yet been measured, it cannot be measured in the absence of a suitable theory of value. A formula for the measurement of the cross-market supply-and-demand relationship should be designed. That requirement is addressed in chapter 5.

Excessive Competition, and Monopoly

Competition is a peculiar phenomenon; it can be good or bad. If the competitive pressure is compared with the atmospheric pressure, it becomes easier to define. We breathe easily in a pressure of one atmosphere. At high aircraft altitudes, the pressure may equal one-half atmosphere. Adaptation or pressurization is required. At low diving depths, the pressure may attain two atmospheres. Slow adaptation, followed by slow decompression are needed. For all common purposes, the optimum pressure is one atmosphere.

Similarly, competitive pressure varies. The horizontal pressure among sellers can attain a coefficient of 2 in a buyers' market or of ½ in a sellers' market. A pressure equal to 1 is neutral; it is optimum because it promotes the largest volume of transactions. A competitive pressure of 1 simply signifies that for every unit offered for sale on a given market at a price equaling the economic value of goods, one unit is demanded; or, vice-versa, that for every unit demanded at that price, one unit is supplied. But that assessment refers only to a single market.

The cross-stage analysis requires a high degree of sophistication. It is possible, even likely, that the competitive pressure remains for protracted periods of time above neutral—in other words, excessive. It reflects a shortage of purchasing power in terms of the production capacity. This presents a social problem inasmuch as excessive competition reduces the volume of possible exchanges and slows the momentum of business activity.

Entrepreneurs besieged by a chronic situation of excessive competition retaliate by seeking monopolistic protection. There are many forms of monopoly, some de facto ownerships of land, raw materials, facilities, trade secrets, and so forth, some sanctioned by patents, trademarks, and copyrights; some are frowned upon by antitrust agencies and some are fraudulent. With chronic excessive competitive pressure and the ensuing race toward monopolistic safety, a problem is created that affects the community as a whole and deserves serious attention.

International Trade Barriers

The early classics advocated international free trade, and even today many economists and statesmen subscribe in theory to that principle, although protective tariffs are hard to forgo in practice. Trade barriers are an expanded version of legalized monopoly. In a world where excessive competitive pressure prevails, they are almost unavoidable.

For international relations to be of permanent mutual benefit, each partner country must first bring competitive pressure under control at home. Then it no longer needs to look to foreign markets as dumping grounds for its surplus. It can approach neighboring states as a friend rather than an enemy. With neutral competitive pressure within every nation, monopolies of all types, including international trade barriers, can safely be dismissed.

Overproduction and Unemployment

Temporary and localized overproduction is common and presents no problem of national concern. But widespread and enduring saturation of consumer markets is an indication of inefficiency in the system. General overproduction is a paradox. It may be only a symptom of underproduction at inflated prices. Regardless of its interpretation, it is in need of explanation and prevention.

Except for local, limited-duration, and frictional unemployment, an explanation is needed for unemployment, underemployment, exaggerated work loads, and deficient pay. Stagnation, one component of stagflation, and unemployment, its acute manifestation, should be prevented.

Business Cycles

Inflation, another component of stagflation, and its antagonist, deflation, alternate in the classical business cycle. Whether or not the government permits deflation, the underlying phenomenon is identical. The voluminous literature on business-cycle theory needs to be supplemented by an explanation of the prime cause of economic instability, and the entire process should be permanently halted.

Overlap of Stagnation and Instability

By definition, stagnation and instability are neither exactly complementary nor entirely compatible. In part the two concepts overlap; in part they are mutually exclusive. Stagnation, however, can be superimposed on all four phases of the business cycle. Even at the peak of prosperity, the productivity of human effort and the utilization of resources may remain below its potential level. Thus understood, stagnation and instability epitomize the essence of modern economic ills, which economic theory has not yet fully accounted for and which should be explained and prevented.

There exist many economic problems outside of stagnation and instability. They are recognized and deserve attention. One thing is certain: they are made much more intractable by stagnation and instability, and their control will be greatly facilitated when the latter are prevented. It is partly for their sake that stagflation and its components should be explained and conquered.

The Speculative-Production Hypothesis

Einstein advocated the hypothesis approach. In 1939, years before his recommendation came to my attention, I postulated the following hypothesis:

> In a multistage economy, speculative production and distribution, initiated in anticipation of the future consumer demand (even if all predictions were always 100 percent correct, and profits always maximized), may have ultimate consequences harmful to the economy by interfering with the free operation of the price mechanism.

The corollary of that hypothesis is: "In a multistage economy, nonspeculative production, by avoiding such interference, may prevent the harmful consequences."

At the time I formulated the hypothesis, I did not know what the consequences might be or how much harm could be prevented by avoiding anticipatory production. After seven years of research, the harm was identified with economic stagnation and instability. The hypothesis appeared justified. The corollary became packed with meaning. By avoiding speculative production, could one really hope to eliminate unemployment and business cycles?

That may not be so hard to believe when one considers that market uncertainty relating to the future consumer demand in terms of costs is completely eliminated through nonspeculative production—that is, production and distribution initiated exclusively in response to prior consumer orders.

The hypothesis guided every step of the research, avoiding time-consuming explorations into blind alleys and providing a constant frame of reference:

nonspeculative production. I found that all eighteen objectives can be satisfied in theory by nonspeculative production.

It is the combination of speculative production and multistage operation that carries a penalty. We can remove the former or the latter at our option and hope to prevent the harm. An alternate corollary, based on that realization, reads: "In a speculative-production economy, single-stage operation, by avoiding interferences with the free operation of the price mechanism, may prevent harmful consequences from occurring."

A third corollary broadens the scope by postulating the possibility of a practical resolution of the problem: "Harmful consequences can perhaps be prevented if certain precautionary measures, specifically designed for the purpose, are applied in a multistage economy characterized by speculative production and distribution."

Models

The profit-motive theory of unemployment and business cycles uses concepts and models new to economics. Four models are described next. The first three are abstractions not likely to occur in pure form in real life. Models 3 and 4 are used here most frequently for the purpose of comparative analysis.

Model 1: Horizontal Specialization without
Speculative Production

In a homestead community, after the initial stage of complete self-sufficiency and independence, neighbors get together and establish a cooperative effort. At first, surplus goods are made available to others; later surplus goods are purposely produced, with orders being taken in advance for delivery of the goods. This may be called horizontal specialization without speculative production. It involves exchanges, purchases, and sales but no markets. Money is used to facilitate exchanges. Credit is extended. In such a model, there is no inefficiency; economic instability is unknown. Only climatic variations affect macroeconomic behavior.

Model 2: Horizontal Specialization with
Speculative Production

The homestead community now finds it unnecessary to obtain advance commitments from all clients. Excess production continues but is geared to an unknown future demand. Exchanges, purchases, and sales are now conducted on markets, to which are brought stocks of goods produced on speculation. Markets are in parallel, not in series. Transactions occur at prices reflecting supply and demand on each market. Market prices gravitate, as Adam Smith predicted, toward natural prices. Money and credit are used. There is no inefficiency; because Say's Law operates dependably, there is no unemployment; and there are no business cycles. Climatic variations still influence the predominantly agricultural model. This is the model described by classical and neoclassical theory. It does not coincide with a modern, industrial economy and is unrealistic.

Model 3: Vertical Specialization without Speculative Production

The introduction of power-driven machinery for industrial production alters the scenario. Independent firms now practice a vertical division of labor. They specialize in producing materials, parts, subassemblies, or consumer goods or in distributing finished products wholesale or retail. For the sake of greater efficiency, they extend the principle of specialization in depth, not just in width. However, and this may not sound realistic, anticipatory production and distribution is excluded from this third model. There are no markets and no inventories, only order-taking facilities. The purpose of the third model is not to describe reality. It is set up as a frame of reference against which the real economy can be assessed. Model 3, as in the case of the first two models, is efficient, fully utilizes resources, and demonstrates stability. It illustrates a hypothetical, broader reality of which model 4 is but a special case.

Model 4: Vertical Specialization with Speculative Production

Model 4 best describes a modern, industrial economy. It includes a vertical succession of firms and markets, as does model 3, but features in addition speculative production and distribution. This has been the structure and pattern of economic activity since the Industrial Revolution. Model 4 distinguishes itself from all the others in two respects: it depicts the present economy, and it is subject to all of the modern inefficiencies, incomplete utilization of resources, and economic instability that are in need of explanation and prevention. Model 4 is not set up as an example. It portrays the economy in which we live and which is not good enough. By comparing it with model 3, one can identify the bridge that may lead from the former to the latter.

Assumptions

Before attacking the problem of stagflation, we must agree on certain simplifying assumptions, which may save unnecessary complications without
compromising results. Realism is of the essence if true progress is to be
achieved, but not all refinements are pertinent. If the long-neglected succession of firms and markets is incorporated, some of the other features of a
realistic model may safely be omitted.

Laissez Faire

Economists have been frustrated for a long time by their efforts to understand
and control unemployment and business cycles. Many have given up hope.
They have turned to the government for assistance. The governments of many
nations have attempted to steer their economies toward stable growth, but it
is questionable whether these economies have really benefited from being
managed.

It would seem logical to turn to those responsible for stagnation and
instability: the entrepreneurs, whether producers or distributors. They cannot
be blamed for modern economic ills, however, because economic theorists
have not explained to them how they generate inefficiencies in the system.
Yet they must change their harmful habits and adopt safe and sound practices.
Recourse to the government is not the route to pursue. While judgment is
reserved as to the optimum role of the state in managing the economy in future
generations, no government intervention is required in the explanation of the
problems at hand or in their resolution. It appears safe to assume a laissez-
faire or hands-off policy on the part of the government.

Sovereignty of Demand and Costs

The chief purpose of economic activity is to satisfy the consumer demand
efficiently. Whether the consumer demand is wise or most beneficial must not
be questioned by the economist. It is an educational concern. Let the economist devise means for meeting efficiently the consumer demand, whatever it
may be.

The consumer demand is the first of two poles of the economic universe.
The second is cost. The entire economic drama is played within that domain.
The axis represents the chain of transactions from raw materials to consumers.
The demand and costs are not, however, those that can be observed and measured on any one market. The actual consumer demand is not the prime
demand; being influenced by stagnation and instability, it is a deviated consumer demand. Actual costs are not prime costs; they too are deviated costs.

The prime consumer demand and prime costs are the poles of the economic universe. They are true independent variables, the sovereignty of which is not to be challenged by the economist.

The second assumption is, then, unquestioned loyalty to demand and cost as primary data.

Free Competition

Imperfect competition has been blamed for causing business cycles. In reality, it plays a role in amplifying stagnation once generated. Analysis shows that the race toward monopoly is caused by excessive competitive pressure and that lessening the pressure may relieve the urge for monopolistic protection. Imperfect competition plays no part in explaining the prime causes of either stagnation or instability.

The third assumption, therefore, is that free competition prevails at all times on all markets.

Perfect Knowledge and Foreknowledge

There has been such heavy emphasis in the economic literature on the importance of information in dealing with equilibrium and stability that we must lay to rest that fragile assumption with a counterassumption. It is assumed that all entrepreneurs always possess perfect knowledge and perfect foreknowledge. At the same time, this defuses the assumption about expectations acting as destabilizing feedback mechanisms.

Profit Maximization

Much confusion exists about profit as a business incentive and about its maximization. The concept has been attacked as unrealistic. There may be more than one explanation to the controversy. Imperfect competition may at times lend so much leeway to large firms that they can pursue less relevant objectives with impunity. Not every firm is set up to measure at frequent intervals profit margins for its principal products. The executive may find it easier to base management decisions on sales volume, market share, or cash flow as surrogates.

The literature claims that entrepreneurs are not actually guided by profit margins. Perhaps businessmen have found from experience that close attention to the profit margin does not help noticeably to induce desirable adjustments or to equate supply and demand in the pipeline. This may be only a vague feeling never made explicit. Also, in the short run, with prices and profit margins fluctuating nervously, it is difficult to recognize an underlying trend that may be significant and worth heeding. Furthermore the signals given by profit margins may not be reliable. This might well explain the low esteem in which the profit margin is held. The overriding importance of the profit is always brought home to the entrepreneur in a recession when the viability of the firm is threatened.

There are several ways of computing profit. Should all sources of corporate profit be included, or only profit from regular operations? Is profit to be computed in terms of investment or simply of transactions? What time period (short run or long run) should be selected? What accounting method (FIFO or LIFO) should be preferred? The concept used here is profit determined, over any convenient period, by the net income from sales, minus variable costs, minus a prorated portion of fixed costs. That is the profit in need of maximization.

Because failure to maximize profits has been erroneously suspected of generating business cycles, it is assumed here that all profits are at all times maximized.

Fixed Capital Investments

Among the many proposed explanations of the business cycle, the most prevalent are the overinvestment theories. The acceleration principle in particular focuses on the relationship between variations in the consumer demand and those, amplified, in the construction of facilities and manufacture of equipment and other producer goods. All of these explanations are superficial. They only push further back the phenomenon to be explained: Why does the consumer demand vary?

The financial tier of the economy is not stressed here because it sheds no light on the deeper problems of the physical economy of raw materials, merchandise in process, and consumer goods. It is assumed that fixed capital investments are there to serve the physical economy, not the reverse. It seems safe to bypass them as possible elements in the explanation of the prime causes of economic instability. They are here assumed neutral.

Exogenous Factors

Other economic factors can be overlooked without affecting the theoretical development or preventive program. They are extraneous to the explanation of the inefficient fulfillment of the consumer demand. They include the irregularities of crops and other meteorological phenomena; the discovery and exhaustion of natural resources; shocks to the economy originating from without; major changes in technology and in processing methods; and changing trends in consumer wants. Many economic problems exist, but unless they affect the processes under study, there is no point in burdening the argument with extraneous elements. These are assumed to be irrelevant.

Vertical Marketing Channels

Marketing channels for raw materials, producer goods, and consumer goods take on highly complicated configurations. They can be likened to apple trees. The roots gather raw materials from many sources; the trunk portrays the compound process of manufacture, from milling to assembling; the branches carry finished products to wholesale outlets; the twigs, to retail establishments; and the apples are the consumer goods.

In this complex flow, there are some fairly stable relationships, with repeat business transacted between established suppliers and loyal clients. But there are also frequent switches from one supplier to his competitor and from one client to another. The ultimate consumer is often totally unaware of the route taken by the article he buys. Despite the tremendous diversity of paths, one fact remains constant: marketing channels always begin at the source of raw materials and always extend to retail displays. Regardless of the particular passage chosen by a given product, it has traversed a succession of stages and markets and is the result of a chain of transactions linking the ultimate consumer to raw-material producers.

Despite their wide diversity, all marketing channels can be represented by pipelines and are here conceptualized as the economic pipeline. That simplifying assumption appears justified.

Economies of Scale

At times producers and distributors are confronted with the dilemma of having to curtail output versus increasing it to reduce costs. Although the inclusion of economies of scale makes the model more realistic, it does nothing to explain stagnation or instability and can safely be ignored. Or it can simply be assumed that decisions are always optimized for maximum returns.

Elasticity of Supply and Demand

When supply or demand are less than infinitely elastic, and they always are, some otherwise possible transactions may fail to materialize. To be realistic, elasticity should be taken into account. However, the extreme cases are relatively unimportant in the aggregate and may safely be disregarded. It is assumed that both supply and demand are reasonably elastic.

3 Speculative Production Breeds Inefficient Consumer Service

This chapter and the next present the profit-motive theory of unemployment and business cycles. Chapter 3 covers microeconomic aspects only. It describes what are believed prime causes of stagflation and its components. It starts with the recognition that a modern industrial economy has a multistage structure and produces and distributes to a large extent in anticipation of future demand. The chapter traces the consequences of that mode of operation. Meeting the consumer demand is the goal of the economic process. How efficient is that process in a speculative multistage economy? Efficient consumer service is found to be incompatible with present business methods and practices.

Unless businessmen learn to meet the consumer demand in a rational and effectual manner, it may be useless to address stagflation directly. It is for the sake of understanding macroeconomic problems that microeconomic productivity and efficiency must first be assessed. Is the changing consumer demand met with a parallel flow of supplies, and are consumers served at the lowest possible cost? This chapter shows how none of the great Western industrial nations now fully achieves that objective.

Chapter 4 relates the findings developed in chapter 3 to an underlying tendency toward stagnation and instability and then to the macroeconomic phenomena of unemployment, business cycles, and stagflation. Together these two chapters cover the whole argument of why stagflation is the penalty of speculative production in a multistage economy.

The Price Mechanism and Prerequisites for Its Unimpeded Operation

The microeconomic analysis is concerned primarily with self-adjusting mechanisms of the economy. These are the pivots of efficient economic activity. If they should fail to operate reliably, the consequences could be manifold and alarming. Producers, distributors, financiers, and consumers would all stand to lose.

There exist several self-adjusting mechanisms in the economy. The price mechanism is the first and most basic lever in economics. It goes much beyond the mere equation of supply and demand on a given market. What are the prerequisites for its dependable operation?

What is found in textbooks usually concerns a single market, but there may be no major problem on a single market. The price mechanism works smoothly and efficiently. It acts like a feedback device, gauging the respective schedules of supply and demand and equating the latter by means of a price adjustment. Except for the consideration of price elasticity of both supply and demand and the imperfection of competition, that is almost all that textbooks have to say about the price mechanism. Not only is such an analysis limited to a single market, it is completely static. Both markets and time are telescoped.

The Price Mechanism in Space and Time

A multistage economy involves a vertical succession of markets. The price mechanism must operate effectively throughout the multimarket pipeline. Vertical intermarket activities, such as the flow of supply from one market to the next or the transmission of the consumer demand from one market to the preceding market are coordinated by the price mechanism. In-depth, or cross-market, coordination is much more important and much more difficult to achieve than is the equation of supply and demand on a single market.

In addition to cross-market coordination of various phenomena, the price mechanism is depended on to coordinate successive and dynamic actions across time. For that purpose, the traditional, static, supply-and-demand schedules are inadequate. Dynamic supply-and-demand comparisons involve the assessment of comparative velocities. Henceforth schedules must be replaced by flows—the flow of supply and the flow of demand. Static equilibria must be replaced by the dynamic synchronization of speeds. These speeds need not be constant; they should move parallel to one another.

The speed of the flow of supply and the speed of demand are of different essences. In the case of the supply, it is the speed with which tangible commodities flow through marketing channels; in the case of the demand, it is the speed with which an invisible dearth develops. The flow of goods and the dearth do not race with one another; the purpose is not for one to outdo the other. The flow of goods caters to the dearth, and the goal is a continuous parallelism of the two speeds. The dynamic equation of supply and demand is the synchronization of their velocities.

Should the flow of goods fall behind the dearth, some wants would remain unsatisfied. Should the flow of goods overtake the dearth, some units would remain unsold or sell at a sacrifice. Speed conflicts may go on for prolonged periods of time. Unfilled wants or unwanted goods may accumulate unchecked. The two velocities would then denote a lack of synchronism, or asynchronism.

Of paramount importance in defining and comparing the two velocities is price. Unless the price is specified, the speed comparison is devoid of meaning. The price of a consumer good is an attribute just as much as its size, weight, color, or quality. Thus, a size 14 ladies' gown, of red velvet, selling for $40 specifies a good in a way that allows the flow of the supply to be compared with the speed of the demand. Yet that price of $40 may change tomorrow. The same gown may be marked up, or down, at any time. This means that its price, like that of any other merchandise (except postage stamps), is completely elusive, unrelated to any constant value. All prices are arbitrary figures, and there are no standards to which they can be related. Flow speeds of supply and demand, therefore, can never be compared.

That is, no doubt, why the concept of comparative speeds is foreign to economic theory. The price that would make the comparison valid is so variable and so hard to nail down that speed relations are meaningless. But what if a standard of economic value were to be developed whereby each product could be assigned a unique value of its own? Speed comparisons could become feasible and meaningful.

A Standard of Economic Value

A tentative definition of the economic value of goods is *the price at which these tend to sell in an efficient, prosperous, and stable economy*. The means for making an economy efficient, prosperous, and stable are of no concern here. The definition is abstract and hypothetical, but since it is to be used only for theoretical analysis, that is not a drawback. The important requirement is that economic value be defined with mathematical accuracy.

A standard has been established whereby the economic value of goods can be determined. The virtue of the standard consists of removing value from the uncertainty attendant upon stagnation and instability. With such a precisely defined value for each commodity, it becomes possible to make accurate and meaningful speed comparisons. The standard lends a unique firmness to the notion of consumer demand velocity and to that of the speed of the flow of goods at any stage of the economic pipeline. With such a common fulcrum, the two speeds can be compared validly under the most diverse circumstances. Such a capability is essential to an understanding of dynamic intermarket phenomena.

Prerequisites for the Free Operation of the Price Mechanism

In order for the flow of supply and the flow of demand to be coordinated in space and time, there are some very stringent requirements. The price mechanism must relay all price fluctuations, regardless of their origin, to all markets in vertical channels *instantly and accurately*. That is what it does in a nonspeculative economy and what is expected of it even in a speculative economy.

Changes in the consumer demand on the retail market must be relayed to all prior markets, including the raw-material market, in the form of revised dollar offers so that all suppliers can adjust the velocity of their operations to the new demand; the relay has to be instant and accurate. Changes in costs at any stage of production or distribution must be transmitted to all subsequent markets, including the retail market, in the form of revised selling prices so that consumers can adjust the speed of their demand to the new costs; the transmission must be instant and accurate. That is the prerequisite for smooth and effective performance, for efficient consumer service. Any deviation disrupts the synchronization of the flows of supply and demand and the harmonious progress of the economic process. It is wasteful of material, human, and financial resources.

The Three Functions Entrusted to the Price Mechanism

Adjustment of the Demand

When supply and demand are mismatched on a given market, a price fluctuation occurs that balances them. The supply has not been altered; the price movement has affected only the demand, causing the demand to accommodate itself to the existing supply. The demand has been reduced by a price rise to where the supply is sufficient to meet the needs of all who have not withdrawn from the market. Or the demand has been boosted by a drop in price to a point where the last unit of supply finds a buyer.

This first adjustment, which will be called *Function A* of the price mechanism, is highly efficient. It encounters no impediments because a single market is involved. The price takes its cues from the existing supply and the current demand on that market. There is no need for transmitting price movements vertically from one market to another. And so the function, whatever its merit, occurs freely, instantly, and accurately. It can be repeated, reversed, and stopped and will always be ready for new adaptations as needed. Function A is performed dependably. This is true in a realistic, speculative economy, as well as in a nonspeculative one.

The operation of function A has high visibility and is easily observable, measurable, and recordable. It should, however, be kept in mind that the price movement erases a disparity between supply and demand quite irrespectively of its origin and throws no light whatever on its causes.

Adjustment of the Supply

Once function A of the price mechanism has been executed and the demand has been either expanded or rationed, it is desirable for the supply to be modified in turn. That is the case in particular when the first adjustment was not just the result of some minor or temporary imbalance. For the flow of supply to be altered, the price fluctuation that affected the demand must travel all the way back to raw-material markets and stimulate or retard the velocity of the supply from that point on. A number of markets may be involved. That is where a problem is likely to be encountered. In a nonspeculative economy, the transmission of price fluctuations would be instant and accurate, and the resulting adjustment in the supply efficient and reliable. The operation in a speculative economy is different.

In classical and neoclassical economics, it has always been assumed that *Function B* of the price mechanism, or adjustment of the supply, is performed efficiently. This has never been proved, so the assumption is subject to reappraisal. In the event of dysfunction of the adjustment in the supply, what would take place on the original market? If the supply has not been modified to parallel the demand, the market price may not return to its original level. Or, if the supply-and-demand disparity persists, another price movement instantly brings the demand in line with the existing supply. In most instances the cause of the disparity is unknown and even irrelevant. It can be due to a change in consumer wants, a change in costs, or simply a failure of supply flow to become coordinated with the velocity of the demand. A similar price movement would very effectively erase the mismatch regardless of its cause.

Thus function A of the price mechanism serves more than one purpose: to alter the demand and to conceal the abnormal performance of function B. Because of the concealment by function A, it is never possible to verify how dependably function B is performed. The result is never evident on the surface. That, of course, is the reason why efficiency has always been assumed. However, a succession of markets is involved, and in a speculative economy, efficiency is questionable.

Vertical Allocation and Equilibration of Profit Margins

The most obvious functions of the price mechanism are its immediate impact on demand and its subsequent control of the supply. It thereby doubly influences the supply-and-demand relationship. Even these first two functions have never been described with sufficient realism. The third function, by far the most important, has never even been mentioned in textbooks.

Function C of the price mechanism is the vertical allocation and equilibration of profit margins. In a multistage economy, there is a need for vertical coordination of successive operations leading up to the delivery of consumer goods. Such operations, including the extraction of raw materials, milling, manufacture of parts and subassemblies, assembly, and wholesale and retail distribution, need to conform to the velocity of the consumer demand and to be coordinated in speed among themselves. For proper coordination, it is necessary that these operations be synchronized, the velocity being consistent at successive stages and matching that of the consumer demand as it accrues on the retail market. The vertical synchronization is governed by relative profit incentives at successive stages.

The aggregate profit margin in the consumer's dollar is allocated to successive firms along the pipeline by the price mechanism. This is its third function. The allocation is a delicate process because the synchronization of successive operations requires a high degree of precision in the balance of incentives. The accurate equilibration of profit margins at successive stages proceeds by successive approximations, requiring of the price mechanism the utmost in efficiency and dependability.

The performance of function C is difficult to verify. It is practically impossible to observe and determine whether it operates effectively. If the allocation is not optimum and the velocity of the supply is inaccurately synchronized at successive stages or with the speed of the consumer demand, a price movement of the function A variety can and will erase the mismatch and hide the maladjustment.

Function C of the price mechanism may go awry even when the consumer demand and costs remain constant. This may appear surprising but should be understood. Such is the power of the profit motive that any distortion may lead to waste, confusion, and conflict.

Impediments to the Intermarket Transmission of Price Fluctuations

Since the Industrial Revolution, the best management and marketing practices have been incompatible with rapidly evolving production and distribution methods. The improvement in production and distribution methods has consisted of pushing the division of labor in the direction of vertical specialization and increasing the proportion of business initiated in anticipation of the future consumer demand. This was started over two hundred years ago. Management and marketing practices failed to keep pace with progress and have been unfit, ineffective, and outdated ever since. Were it not for speculative production, such practices might still be adequate today. It is the superimposition of speculative production on antiquated management and marketing practices that throws physical impediments into the transmission channels of price fluctuations. Some examples follow.

Transmission of Retail-Price Fluctuations to Raw-Material Markets

Speculative production and distribution intercepts demand fluctuations in their upstream travels. Retail-price fluctuations are never relayed to raw-material producers through the units first subjected to the fluctuations. These units, in accordance with anticipatory practices, have already been purchased by retailers from manufacturers or wholesalers, and their purchase prices are not subject to renegotiation when sold at retail. Similar interception occurs at the wholesale level and at all prior levels until raw-material markets are reached.

If the upstream relay of retail-price fluctuations is predicated on reorders, they cannot reach raw-material producers with instant dispatch. Consumer items are reordered in wholesale quantities, many at three- or six-month intervals, entailing considerable time lags. The latter are compounded at every stage, with cumulative delays often running into many months. By the time the ripples in the consumer demand have spread to raw-material markets, they are completely out of date with current demand fluctuations. It is safe to conclude that time lags of such proportions may turn into chronic inaccuracies. The signals received by farmers and miners rarely represent current consumer wants.

Consumer-demand fluctuations can use another route in their upstream travels: anticipations by successive firms of what the demand will be when their output is ready to be marketed. Such anticipations concern costs and the demand (product mix, selling prices, and volumes). Time lags are avoided but only at the cost of inaccuracies. Anticipations may be in error. Consider that a firm must anticipate not only the future demand, costs, and prices but the predictions of suppliers, clients, and competitors. The odds are against predictions being consistently accurate. And predictions would have to be correct at all stages, from retailers to raw-material producers. Otherwise the relay of consumer-demand fluctuations, even though timely, would not be accurate.

The worst is that although all predictions at all stages were in fact always completely correct, the transmission of retail-price fluctuations to raw-material producers would still not be accurate. The reason is that the anticipation of future price fluctuations is not the equivalent of the transmission of current fluctuations.

In conclusion, consumer-demand fluctuations are transmitted to raw-material producers either with time lags or inaccurately. And since extended time lags are equivalent to inaccuracies, the latter are the rule rather than the exception.

Transmission of Raw-Material and Intermediate Cost Fluctuations to Retail Markets

Speculative production and distribution veils current raw-material and intermediate cost changes from the consumer. The costs incorporated in the units bought by the consumer are unrelated to current raw-material and intermediate costs. Although selling prices are meaningless, the consumer is unaware of this and bases his plans on them in good faith.

If cost fluctuations are dependent on being transmitted to consumers on the sales tags of the merchandise, the time lag equals in duration the production and distribution cycle. In some instances, as in the case of natural-rubber products, the cycle extends over several years. Substantial time lags may turn into serious inaccuracies.

If the transmission of cost fluctuations is performed by anticipations at successive stages, time is telescoped, but accuracy is sacrificed in the process. And even when all predictions are correct, what is conveyed is anticipated, not current, cost changes. This is not the equivalent of the instant and accurate transmission of current raw-material and intermediate-cost changes to the consumer. The prerequisites of the dependable operation of the price mechanism fail to be met.

Transmission of Price Fluctuations in Both Directions

Several additional impediments prevent the price mechanism from free and efficient operation.

Price setting is a common practice, mainly on retail markets, but also on wholesale markets and even on some commodity markets. It simplifies transactions, especially for low-priced items. Bargaining takes time and requires the presence of principals; it is practiced for large purchase orders. The effect of price setting is to suspend the transmission of price fluctuations upstream and downstream until prices are revised. In many instances, revisions are never made until the stock is exhausted.

Price rigidities are both a cause and an effect. They are the effect of excessive competitive pressure combined with an underlying trend toward economic instability in which inflation induces buyers to hold on to prices once accepted and deflation prompts sellers to grasp prices once obtained. As a cause, price rigidities resist the transmission of price fluctuations upstream and downstream.

The absorption of price fluctuations is a common practice. Some fluctuations merely sway back and forth and need not be forwarded. Others are of minor duration or amplitude. In such instances, absorption is natural and of no consequence. In other cases, where longer and more pronounced price trends are underway, the absorption of fluctuations arrests their transmission in both directions. This results in canceling desirable adjustments.

Quite frequently price fluctuations are absorbed deliberately, for the purpose of stabilizing the price structure. Laudable though the purpose may be, absorption is the surest way to prevent stability. Enduringly stable prices require the free, unhampered operation of a self-adjusting mechanism such as the price system.

If insignificant fluctuations are excluded, whether a cost change is not conveyed to the buyer or a demand change is intercepted in its travels toward suppliers, the practice of absorbing rather than passing on price fluctuations has an inhibiting effect on the vital signal-relaying mission of the price mechanism. Self-adjustment fails to materialize.

Price fluctuations can also be exaggerated on their way to the extreme markets. Time lags and other obstacles to the free propagation of fluctuations may hold back urgently needed adjustments until panic strikes surprised upstream or downstream firms. These are then liable to overreact, exaggerating the original fluctuations and defeating the purpose of instant and accurate transmission of current price fluctuations.

A common merchandising practice that is particularly detrimental is that of certain mail-order houses. A number of these issue annual or semiannual catalogues, and maintain prices until the next edition is distributed. The net effect of that practice is to intercept price fluctuations at the retail level for six to twelve months every year. The paralyzing influence of the system extends even to the suppliers of these houses, who must commit themselves to deliver merchandise for a period of months at the original price. The whole idea of a self-adjusting mechanism is negated by such an arrangement.

There are many other impediments to the free and dependable operation of the price mechanism. Each militates against the attainment of the required instant and accurate transmission of price fluctuations throughout the economic pipeline. In a nonspeculative production economy, none of these impediments would have harmful effects since every transaction would necessarily encompass the entire pipeline from the retail to raw-material markets. All demand and cost fluctuations would be instantly and accurately relayed to the extreme markets. No obstacle would prevent the price mechanism from operating efficiently. All three functions of the price mechanism would be performed reliably. The consumer demand would be met efficiently.

In a speculative-production economy, the many impediments encountered by the price mechanism cripple its action to such an extent that the microeconomic consumer demand can no longer be met effectively and stagflation may well be the ultimate macroeconomic penalty.

Recapitulation of Obstacles to the Free Operation of the Price Mechanism

1. Retail-price fluctuations are never relayed to raw-material producers through the units first subjected to the fluctuations.
2. Retail-price fluctuations, when relayed to raw-material producers through infrequent reorders, reach their destinations with compound time lags.

3. Retail-price fluctuations, when relayed upstream through anticipation of the future demand, costs, prices, product mix, and volumes, reach their destinations with variable degrees of inaccuracy.

4. Raw-material cost fluctuations, when relayed to the retail market through the merchandise, reach their destinations with time lags coextensive with the duration of the production and distribution cycle.

5. Raw-material cost fluctuations, when relayed downstream through anticipation of the future demand, costs, prices, product mix, and volumes, reach their destinations with variable degrees of inaccuracy.

6. Price setting by sellers at any stage may simplify business, but it stands in the way of relaying demand fluctuations toward raw-material markets.

7. Price rigidities, caused by excessive competitive pressure, resist the transmission of price fluctuations toward the extreme markets.

8. The common practice of absorbing rather than communicating price fluctuations intercepts their relay to the extreme markets.

9. The exaggeration of overdue price fluctuations by overreacting firms adds to inaccuracies in relaying price fluctuations.

10. Mail-order houses issuing annual or semiannual catalogues, and expecting manufacturers to guarantee their prices for such intervals, intercept the transmission of price fluctuations in either direction for six to twelve months every year.

With such a barrage of impediments to the instant and accurate relay of price fluctuations up and down each pipeline, the price mechanism cannot be depended upon to perform its vital functions effectively.

Effect of the Impediments on the Performance of the Three Functions

Function A

The first function of the price mechanism involves a single market and therefore does not require intermarket transmission of price fluctuations. Function A, the adjustment of the demand, is essentially effective. Speculative production has no impact on it. The adjustment is subject to the price elasticity of supply and demand, the degree of freedom of competition, and promptness of the market response. The adjustment process is practically immediate, has high visibility, and may be measured without difficulty.

Insofar as its performance reflects a change in demand or in costs, function A is superficial and remains incomplete until supplemented by function B. Together the first two functions respond to changes in the consumer demand and in costs originating anywhere along the economic pipeline. Unfortunately, function B is not performed as easily or effectively as function A.

Function B

Adjustment of the supply involves intermarket processes. It relies upon the transmission of price fluctuations upstream to reach raw-material markets. The impediments preclude dependable performance of function B and with it, efficient adjustment of the supply. Function B of the price mechanism is incompletely or inaccurately discharged. The market price will not return to its original level. Residual supply-and-demand disparities are canceled on the original market through additional price movements of the function A variety. This superficial equation of supply and demand cheats both producers and consumers. Prices fluctuate without reason to conceal incomplete adjustments of the supply.

The extent to which supply is adjusted is difficult to ascertain because of the prompt response of function A to maladjustments. Mismatches are erased regardless of their cause, masking the true underlying unresolved disparities. Measurements are practically impossible.

Function C

The allocation and equilibration of profit margins between successive stages rests entirely on the instant and accurate cross-market transmission of all price fluctuations. The process consists of repeated intermarket profit-margin adjustments until balance is attained. Balanced allocation does not necessarily mean equal profit margins at every stage; for each firm in the pipeline, it means an inducement such that it will operate in synchronism with its suppliers and clients at prices equaling the economic value of goods.

Such a delicate maneuver cannot possibly be executed dependably where the price mechanism is incapacitated in so many ways. Cumulative time lags and inaccuracies in the relay of price changes substantially impair the efficacy of function C.

Whether flashing true or false signals, profit margins continue to govern the velocities with which successive firms produce or distribute. When profit margins are distorted, velocities are imperfectly synchronized with the speeds of prior and/or subsequent operations and with the velocity of the consumer demand. This is the prime cause of inefficient consumer service.

Function C is practically impossible to observe, and results cannot be measured. When it misfunctions, as we must now conclude that it may most of the time, function A price movements promptly erase any supply-and-demand disparities on all affected markets. That action is but superficial in that it does not synchronize the velocity of supply-and-demand flows. It only gives the appearance of equality on every market. And by hiding the unresolved speed conflicts, function A makes it difficult to know whether or to what extent function C has actually been performed.

The resulting confusion and inevitable waste occur before any changes take place in the consumer demand or in costs. When such changes are superimposed on the chronic speed conflicts and are themselves inaccurately or incompletely translated into adjustments by function B, the cumulative disturbances constitute persistent and nonnegligible intermarket disequilibria. Though very real, these are never left exposed on any one market.

When profit margins are inaccurately equilibrated at successive stages, they are likely to be distorted. The multiple impediments to the operation of the price mechanism have the direct effect of distorting most profit margins of most firms for most of their products most of the time.

Impact of the Pricing Policy

The profit margin of a given firm for a given product is a volatile, elusive, and constantly changing residue. It is the difference between income from sales as influenced by consumer-demand fluctuations and total expenditures as affected by raw-material and intermediate cost fluctuations. The income from sales and total expenditures can be likened to the jaws of a vise that squeeze the profit. In a dynamic model, the fluctuating profit margin is a moving differential governed by motions of both jaws of the vise. These can stand still or move in parallel directions, with no change in the profit margin; one can move while the other remains constant, or they can both move in the same direction but by unequal increments, with a corresponding positive or negative change in the profit margin; or the jaws of the vise can move in opposite directions, the profit margin being doubly affected.

Under conditions of imperfect transmission of price fluctuations up and down the economic pipeline, the jaws of the vise inaccurately reflect what goes on at the retail stage and the raw-material stage. The signal may betray the consumer's wishes; the entrepreneur may respond in good faith to the belated and misleading directions it contains.

The degree of distortion of the profit margin is governed to some extent by the pricing policy used by the producer or merchant in buying and selling merchandise. From the standpoint of the distortion of profit margins, there are three distinct pricing policies, plus their variations and combinations.

Shortsighted Pricing Policy

This pricing policy rests, for relaying retail-price fluctuations to raw-material producers, on indirect transmission through reorders. Fluctuations are relayed through units ordered in replacement of those subjected to the fluctuations. For relaying raw-material and intermediate cost fluctuations to consumers, the policy depends on transmission through the flow of supply.

The shortsighted pricing policy consists at each stage, when buying, of taking into account current price fluctuations on the two immediately adjacent markets; when selling, of adding an appropriate target markup to costs incurred. If possible, selling prices are maintained constant until goods are sold. The policy is believed conservative but entails losses during periods of rising as well as periods of falling prices. It is also inefficient.

Considerable and cumulative time lags are the result. The extent of the delays varies at each stage with the mean frequency of reordering, the ratio of the number of suppliers to the number of clients, and the applicable portion of the production and/or distribution cycle.

To the delays must be added various inaccuracies arising from the impediments listed previously. A difficulty peculiar to the transmission of fluctuations through reorders is this: Since the number of units purchased at one time does not correspond to the number of units sold at one time, what portion of a selling-price fluctuation should be transmitted through the next reorder? Suppose 450 units were sold at $20 each, but the next 50 had to be sold at $16; it is now time to reorder 1,000 units. What decrease in the ordering price should be sought (assuming that prices are subject to bargaining)? There is no mathematical formula for computing the answer. Who knows whether a fluctuation is temporary or permanent or what further fluctuations may occur? The transmission through reorders is anything but certain or dependable. To the substantial time lags must be added at each stage a nonnegligible element of inaccuracy.

Profit margins under the shortsighted pricing policy may be distorted most of the time at every stage, and the degree of distortion is likely to vary from one stage to another.

Speculative-Pricing Policy

Under this policy, prices offered for merchandise are based on anticipated raw-material and intermediate cost changes and on the estimated future consumer demand for the period over which the merchandise is expected to be sold on the retail market. Selling prices, first set at a corresponding markup, are periodically revised to maximize profits as market conditions change.

Under the speculative-pricing policy, profit-margin distortions could theoretically fall to zero. The protracted time lags in the transmission of retail-price fluctuations to raw-material producers are telescoped. Raw-material and intermediate cost fluctuations, instead of flowing at the speed of the production and distribution cycle, are transmitted instantly. But the policy comprises an element of prediction, always hazardous because even the most intricate calculations can be defeated by errors of judgment of the entrepreneur's suppliers, clients, or competitors. When that happens, the profit margins of all parties are distorted.

The worst feature of the speculative-pricing policy is that even when all predictions by all concerned are always correct, profit margins are still likely to be distorted because prediction of the future consumer demand and future costs is not equivalent to the instant transmission of current consumer-demand fluctuations and current cost changes.

A variation of the speculative-pricing policy consists of basing prices offered for merchandise on anticipated cost changes on the supplier market and on the estimated future demand on the client market. While easier to apply, that variation is even less accurate. The entrepreneur is at the mercy of his suppliers' and clients' judgment of future costs and prices.

To summarize, the speculative-pricing policy seems to eliminate the sizable time lags involved in the shortsighted policy and thus to resolve the problem. But it has two drawbacks: the probability that some agents predict erroneously the future demand in terms of costs and the certainty that even when all agents' predictions are always correct, these predictions are not the equivalent of the instant and accurate transmission of current demand and cost fluctuations.

Synchronized-Pricing Policy

Under this policy, parties to transactions take their price clues from current fluctuations in the consumer demand, as well as in raw-material and intermediate costs. Thus price fluctuations are synchronized on all markets. The pricing policy conforms to the prerequisites for the free operation of the price mechanism in general and for the instant and accurate transmission of all price fluctuations in particular. Yet it is rarely applied today. It may not be evident to an entrepreneur that such a pricing policy may have special merits.

The synchronized-pricing policy goes a long way toward avoiding profit-margin distortions, but it is not quite sufficient. Every time the moment of the sale of a unit does not coincide with the moment of its purchase (or the purchase of a set of component parts), the consumer demand, or costs, or both, may have changed during the interval, the differential between income and expenditures may be altered, and the profit margin distorted. Nevertheless, of the three policies, the synchronized-pricing policy is the most reliable and the most efficient.

Distorted Profit Margins Cause Chronic
Supply-and-Demand Disparities

The crucial importance of the profit motive in all economics and business cannot be overemphasized. Without the inducement of profit, the entire private economy would quickly come to a halt. In addition, the relative size of the profit margin acts to allocate scarce resources where consumers indicate they are wanted most. Thus, profit margins are the strings whereby marionettes are actuated on the stage of economics. The marionettes' every move is dictated by the hand that holds the strings. Profit margins being the most potent force known in economics, it is surprising that they have had practically no place in economic theory of any school.

Because of their potency, profit margins ought to be closely analyzed, for if anything goes wrong with them, the consequences might be calamitous. In fact something has gone wrong with them; distorted profit margins are a serious problem, capable of generating severe consequences.

The immediate effect of distorted profit margins is the inducement of a flow of supply systemically out of phase with itself. Successive operations are not only not synchronized, they are caused to proceed at conflicting speeds. On every market, supply and demand, to be equated, require price movements. Such movements only give the appearance of equation; the flow remains unsynchronized. More mismatches are produced with every day that passes and are cumulative.

Stable supply-and-demand equality results from operations synchronized by undistorted profit margins. No price fluctuations are needed because equation has already been achieved. Where no price fluctuations are needed, price stability reigns. In real life, these potent levers work in reverse. Profit margins are distorted; supply and demand are continually mismatched. Price fluctuations take place on every market. The price structure becomes unstable.

The synchronization of supply-and-demand velocities requires the allocation of profit margins in balanced proportions at successive stages. The resulting synchronization does not mean that supply and demand have to remain constant; it means that the supply faithfully follows changes in the demand, and demand conforms to changing costs. Although both velocities may vary, their motions are parallel.

Another remark pertains to the relative potency of demand and cost changes and the allocation of profit margins. When demand or costs change, an adjustment is called for, but this may be a one-time occurrence. Even if function B is not performed effectively, the consequence is limited. A price movement erases the supply-and-demand mismatch, and all is forgotten. But once profit margins have been misallocated, they are likely to remain misallocated. They then have a dynamic and recurring effect. Distorted profit margins generate continual and cumulative mismatches that are never completely resolved. Even a minor distortion has a constantly growing detrimental impact.

Social and Ethical Implications

Basic Business Dilemma

Profit-margin distortions raise a dilemma for the entrepreneur that he cannot elude: either he maximizes his distorted profits and produces chronic and systematic cross-market supply-and-demand disparities or he equates supply and demand and sustains losses or earns reduced profits. Should he be public-spirited enough to accept certain sacrifices in order to attain and preserve supply-and-demand equality, he would not know whether or when supply equals demand or whether or to what extent he should accelerate or slow down his output. Thus, inaccurate as it is, the maximization of profits remains the only guide toward equating supply and demand.

Without the entrepreneur's being aware of the origin of the difficulty, the wastes to which profit-margin distortions give rise produce hostility between agents who participate in the business process. Because of conflicting speeds between the flow of goods at various stages of the pipeline and the rate of the consumer demand, continual antagonisms arise on every market between suppliers and clients. Even at the heart of an individual firm, a growing resentment builds up between management eager for profits and the wage earner whose raison d'être and remuneration is predicated upon efficient satisfaction of the consumer demand. Thus the business dilemma between the maximization of profits and the equation of supply and demand may be at the root of the conflict between capital and labor, at the root of the class struggle, at the root of communist revolution.

The answer to the problem is to organize the marketing phases of the production and distribution process so that the entrepreneur's natural incentive, the profit margin, remains undistorted and, when maximized, tends to synchronize supply and demand. The interest of the individual will then coincide with that of the social group. Such a solution will appeal directly to the selfish instincts of human nature and make entrepreneurs perform the actions that will most benefit the entire community.

The Twin Problems of Business

By tradition entrepreneurs have striven to meet the consumer demand. They have assumed that it is both legitimate and efficient, in pursuing that goal, to seek maximum profits. Data gathering and accurate forecasts have been held essential ingredients for profit maximization. Some analysts believe that, given perfect foreknowledge, businessmen could achieve complete economic efficiency, assure the highest utilization of resources, and avoid booms and depressions.

They have been aware of the first only of two problems of private enterprise:

1. How to operate so as to maximize profits, and

2. How to make certain that, when profits are maximized, supply is equated to demand.

The second objective, the attainment of which has been taken for granted, is a basic problem of private enterprise, along with, and equal in importance to, the first problem.

Knowledge is a servant to motivation. When they conflict, as they frequently do because they travel through different channels, the incentive, not knowledge, invariably governs the entrepreneur's actions. Even a distorted incentive outranks correct information.

The need for supply-and-demand equation has never been acknowledged because of the difficulty in measuring the static and dynamic supply-and-demand relationship. And if the maximization of profits remains the only guide toward equating supply and demand, the entrepreneur has no choice but to continue operating as he always has.

**Chronic Supply-and-Demand Mismatches Breed
Inefficient Consumer Service**

Efficiency in meeting the consumer demand is ruled out by the series of impediments to the free operation of the price mechanism. Nothing other than the price mechanism can ensure efficient consumer service. If permitted, the price mechanism would do so by allocating profit margins in balanced proportions to successive firms. Balanced profit margins would induce a supply flow synchronized with itself at various stages and with the velocity of the consumer demand. A synchronized flow would mean continual supply-and-demand equality without the need for function A–type price movements. That kind of equality is true equality, obtained from within, and is likely to remain stable. It permits the largest volume of transactions. It also allows the optimum utilization of material, human, and financial resources. For these reasons, it is synonymous with economic efficiency.

When supply and demand flow at conflicting rates of speed because of profit-margin distortions, the actual volume of output remains inevitably below the potential volume. The following example provides an explanation.

Let the marketing channel linking the raw-material producer to the consumer be compared with an industrial assembly line. Some of the rules that apply to an assembly line apply also to the marketing channel. For example, highest efficiency is reached when work performed at successive stations of the assembly line is synchronized as accurately as possible. This is accomplished wherever feasible through mechanical devices such as gears with appropriate ratios, and through time-and-motion studies on the basis of which optimal team work sequences are established. Thus the speed of the line is controlled, and accurate synchronization of all operations is assured.

Should one operation exceed the overall speed of the line, some units would go to waste, or someone's time would not be fully occupied. Should one operation be performed at a velocity inferior to that of the rest, it would reduce the output of the entire assembly line to its speed. Suppose that the overall speed of the line is one hundred units per day but one operation contributes only ninety units per day; no more than ninety complete, assembled units can issue from the line.

So it is with the economic pipeline. Successive stages specialized in agricultural, processing, mining, milling, manufacturing, and marketing operations contribute to the delivery of finished products to the consumer. In this line, too, the secret of efficiency is accurate synchronization. Synchronization in this case is not assured by mechanical gears; it is achieved through the incentive provided by the profit. If each firm in the pipeline is allocated just the right proportion of the overall profit, it can operate in coordination with the other firms and achieve synchronization of its flow with everyone else's flow.

That is not what takes place in a speculative economy. The price mechanism that might ensure synchronization is hindered from carrying out function C efficiently. As a result, some firms in the channel are overstimulated and others understimulated. One firm—that which receives the lowest stimulation from its profit margin—is the slowest. It forms the bottleneck; its velocity limits the output of the entire pipeline. The aggregate output cannot exceed that of the slowest member of the team. As for the rest of the firms, their output in excess of that of the slowest is at least partially wasted. If a substitute use can be found for their excess output, a portion of the gross waste can be recovered. This is not the picture of the highest possible efficiency of production and distribution. Unfortunately the waste is continual and finally reaches nonnegligible proportions.

What is the effect of the compound waste on the fulfillment of the consumer demand? The consuming public can never receive the potential volume of goods that producers and distributors could make available with existing facilities. It is all a problem of cross-stage coordination of incentives. Under the circumstances, it cannot be claimed that the consumer demand is met efficiently.

4

Inefficient Consumer Service Breeds Stagflation

In a speculative multistage economy, a string of impediments prevents the price mechanism from adjusting supply and demand with accuracy. The price mechanism also fails to allocate profit margins to successive firms in balanced proportions. Continual supply-and-demand disparities resulting from incomplete adjustments and from distorted profit margins are promptly obscured on every market by price fluctuations. This may explain why they have not been suspected before.

Because of conflicting rates of operating speeds at successive stages, the actual output of each pipeline falls short of the potential output. Chronic waste takes place. The consumer demand is not fulfilled with economic efficiency. This chapter demonstrates how a lack of efficiency in serving the consumer translates into stagflation.

From Inefficient Consumer Service to Stagnation

Several steps are involved in describing how economic inefficiency in meeting the consumer demand may lead to stagnation.

Reduced Output and Increased Unit Costs

Imbalanced profit margins at successive stages tend to induce conflicting velocities in the flow of supply; some stages overperform and others underperform. In each pipeline, one stage, that which receives the least stimulus from its profit margin, forms the bottleneck. Aggregate output of the pipeline is limited to the velocity of the bottleneck.

Excess output of other operations is at least partially wasted. At times alternate uses can be found for oversupply, but there is an effort, a shift, and a cost involved in adapting and redirecting surplus goods.

Meanwhile consumers have been cheated out of units they could and would have acquired. Suppose a given pipeline is capable of turning out 100 units per week, to sell for $20 each. Some operators produce as many as 110 component parts, and the slowest operator on the pipeline puts out only 90 units. All that consumers can ever get is 90 units per week. All parts produced and distributed in excess of 90 are partially wasted because they do not match the output of other stages of the pipeline. Therefore they must be paid for just as much as those units that are integrated into complete finished products. As much time and effort have been expended as would have been necessary for the entire output of 100 units. Thus the total cost for 90 units is no less, and the cost per unit is more.

It is clear that if the cost of providing 100 complete units is spread over the 90 units actually offered the consumer, unit costs are increased by one-ninth, or 11.11 percent. The new unit cost is $20 \times 100/90$, or \$22.22. If the consuming public buys the 90 units offered at \$22.22, it will use up the totality of the funds destined for the 100 units, but 10 percent of the consumer wants, though paid for, will go unfilled, and the 90 percent will be overpriced. Fewer goods are offered at inflated prices.

Waste of Resources and Waste of Purchasing Power

When the actual output remains short of the potential output, some waste is unavoidably generated. The waste is, first, a waste of material resources: those that exceed the output of the bottleneck operation. It also involves human resources: the labor that goes to naught because parts do not match. Financial resources are wasted: the investment is less efficient than it could be. All of these wastes are continuous and therefore cumulative.

But the worst form of waste that occurs when profit margins are distorted and supply and demand are improperly synchronized is a waste of consumer purchasing power. For a given income, the consuming public cannot obtain a full measure of the goods wanted at prices equaling the economic value of goods. Regardless of the price paid, the total quantity can never exceed the output of the slowest operator in the pipeline. This sets a ceiling on the purchasing power of the buying population.

Who says consumer purchasing power says purchasing power of the currency. The two are synonymous.

It is important to distinguish between the absolute level of purchasing power and purchasing power in relation to the nation's production and distribution capacity. When an improvement in production and/or distribution processes reduces the cost of goods to consumers, the consumer purchasing power is increased, but not in relation to the potential production and distribution capacity of the nation because the latter has been increased as well. The reverse is symmetrical. Failure to modernize with more efficient equipment is a form of waste. Consumers receive fewer goods than could be produced but not fewer goods than can be produced with existing facilities. The purchasing power is not less in terms of the nation's capacity to produce.

Waste of the type discussed here is of a different essence. An output restricted to the velocity of the slowest operation in the pipeline represents a waste of purchasing power not only absolutely but also in relation to the nation's production capacity, which remains undiminished.

When purchasing power is considered in relation to the nation's production capacity, it is indeed a scarce commodity. It has been contended that it cannot be created. It can be shared among segments of the population. It can also be borrowed from future taxpayers. Or, it can be wasted. The most effective way to increase purchasing power is to stop wasting it. It may thus be restored to its full potential level, which equals the production capacity of the nation, as claimed by Jean-Baptiste Say.

When the aggregate purchasing power equals a nation's production capacity, there are no ceilings to markets. The supply creates its own demand. That is why, in a modern, industrial economy, in which a nonnegligible fraction of the potential purchasing power is wasted and the remaining consumer demand is further affected by sales resistance, it can be said that: *The largest untapped market in the world is reclaimable purchasing power.* It knows no limits.

Sales Resistance and Need for a Sales Effort

In a vertically specialized economy, the bulk of production and distribution activities proceed through economic pipelines. A phenomenon that necessarily affects the pipeline is common to all pipelines and has an impact on the economy at large. The phenomenon is the microfoundation of nationwide macroeconomic behavior.

If the phenomenon is favorable to each pipeline, it is bound to affect favorably the economy as a whole. If the phenomenon is deleterious to each pipeline, it will produce nationwide economic disturbances and malaise. These cannot be explained through other macroeconomic processes. Unless they are related to their microfoundations, they remain unexplained and incomprehensible.

It is not to be expected that output can be reduced and unit costs increased in every pipeline without some reaction by the consuming public. Every item on retail shelves is now priced higher, but buyers do not know why. Thus a portion of the population goes unsatisfied, and the rest pay higher prices than would otherwise be necessary.

In time the public may become suspicious, resentful, or resistant. Some clients may decide they would rather make certain goods themselves or do without. Thus the unit of marginal subjective utility is reached before all existing units are sold. The total cost must now be spread over an even lesser number of units. The price may go higher still, causing another notch of resistance. This applies to everything the consumer buys and may explain the origin of sales resistance.

The entrepreneur must acknowledge sales resistance as a fact of life. His response is a sales effort that might never have been needed. Sales are pushed through market surveys, product differentiation, publicity, new customer services, and sales promotion.

Additional manpower is needed to conduct a constant sales effort. Assuming initial full employment, that manpower can be recruited only from production and distribution teams. An additional slice of total output must be sacrificed, representing a further reduction in output without a corresponding saving in cost. Total expenditures must now be spread over an even smaller number of units, with the result that unit prices are again increased, and sales resistance is intensified. Even a comparatively minor original waste is compounded so that the consumer is made to pay more and more for fewer and fewer goods. These are the ingredients that generate the continual and costly need for pushing sales instead of simply meeting an insatiable consumer demand.

The waste of consumer purchasing power and the customers' reluctance to buy overpriced goods, both of which are due directly and solely to an insufficient output of finished goods, paradoxically result in overproduction or an incomplete utilization of material, human, and financial resources.

In conclusion, it may be stated that when we learn to equilibrate profit margins at all stages, we may never want to produce or market such quantities as will be needed to exceed the effective demand.

Market Uncertainty and Uncertainty of Income

If the effective consumer demand were insatiable, business as a whole would be a winning proposition. Competence, judgment, and capital would be the only requirements for business success. Selling would be the least of concerns; it would be reduced to receiving payments and taking orders. The economy could be stable and prosperous.

An illustration of the economic atmosphere in which business would be conducted is borrowed from the experience of consumers during World War II. The civilian population, subjected to many restrictions, was unable to buy luxuries and even many items considered necessities. Since this was a sellers' market, goods produced and marketed for civilian consumption required no sales effort. Many sales people, advertising personnel, display specialists, and others could be released to join the ranks of factory workers.

Anyone who had anything to sell found an eager applicant willing to make special efforts—stand in line, pay cash in advance, give up many traditional customer services—in order to obtain the goods. Admittedly this was an abnormal situation of scarcity coupled with full employment and high incomes. Nevertheless, from the standpoint of the degree of sales resistance and the need for a sales effort, it imparted a feeling for what a more normal buyer-seller relation might be in a peacetime economy. If purchasing power equaled the production capacity and competitive pressure were neutral, the selling function might be reduced to that of a cashier and order taker.

In a real, modern industrial economy, doing business is a daily struggle. A lack of purchasing power combined with sales resistance does not permit the totality of goods to be sold profitably; the mathematics of the situation opposes it. But for the extra sales effort of producers and distributors, business as a whole might be a losing proposition. As it is, the real loser is probably the consumer, who pays higher prices for the privilege of buying overabundant goods.

General overproduction creates for the entrepreneur a situation where there is no assurance that all units produced can be sold at a profit. Unavoidably the situation generates an atmosphere of market uncertainty. One thing is certain: not all units of all goods can be sold at prices yielding a profit, but no one can tell which units of what goods will be unprofitable. Market uncertainty poses a threat to every business firm in the nation. It is the most insidious form of economic uncertainty and gives rise to a sizable portion of the entrepreneurial profit.

Market uncertainty is at the root of financial uncertainty. No equity-type investment can be more secure than the business firm or business operations it finances. Financial uncertainty is essentially the result, not the cause, of market uncertainty.

Together market uncertainty and financial uncertainty generate uncertainty of income for workers and investors. How can a job be secure when company profits are not, and how can the yield of investments be free of risk when the firms financed are not?

The explanation of market uncertainty and uncertainty of income is a dearth of goods, and inflated prices. Neither form of uncertainty will yield to any measure short of the recovery of wasted purchasing power through closer synchronization of supply and demand flows.

Excessive Competitive Pressure, Price Rigidity, and the Pursuit of Monopoly

Speculative production in a multistage economy leads to a whole chain of consequences. When the purchasing power of the consuming public has been eroded and inflated prices have generated sales resistance, every entrepreneur must vie with his competitors for markets. Under other circumstances he might have considered other businessmen in the same line as his collaborators rather than rivals. Now, he has to fight to retain his share of the market.

This situation is characterized by excessive competitive pressure in which high competition among sellers is not offset by low competition among buyers. A price movement merely equalizes the two horizontal competitions but fails to bring down either to unity. While competition is good, an excess of it is counterproductive. As long as purchasing power is sufficient to buy what the nation is capable and willing to produce, competition remains or returns to neutral; the maximum volume of transactions can take place; there is no overall sales resistance or general market saturation. But when purchasing power goes to waste, outlets are scarce. One supplier can sell out in a market only at the expense of another. That is meant at prices equaling the economic value of goods.

Excessive competitive pressure affects the fluidity of prices and wages. When sellers find their profits squeezed by markets that are becoming saturated, they are reluctant to lower their selling prices, despite overabundant merchandise. When buyers feel the profit squeeze because of a scarcity of goods at acceptable prices, they resist bidding higher prices despite dwindling supplies. As a result, the volume of transactions always falls off rather than prices moving up or down. This may explain price rigidities. And when labor-management relations experience similar excessive pressures, the reluctance of workers to accept lower pay and that of employers to consent higher rates leads to layoffs or strikes rather than compensation adjustments. This may explain wage rigidities.

Price and wage rigidities are unfortunate in that they impede the normal operation of self-adjusting mechanisms and reduce overall efficiency. They would not occur in a nonspeculative economy where purchasing power equals the production capacity. In an inflationary economy, rigidities are mostly downward, with the same results of slowing transactions and reducing productivity.

Excessive competitive pressure threatens the entrepreneur's profits. It is only natural that he should seek protection. Protection is afforded by law. For specified periods, patents, trademarks, and copyrights confer exclusive rights and privileges to their holders in recognition of novel creations. The purest form of monopoly is the ownership of land with unique advantages, such as oil or other mineral deposits, or sole sources of raw materials. Further legal means of protection are common in marketing programs: product differentiation, publicity playing on customers' emotions, and a host of other monopolistic practices, ethical or otherwise. In addition, many measures may run counter to the antitrust laws administered by the Justice Department and the Federal Trade Commission.

Every form of monopoly puts a brake on the economy because it thrives on a scarcity of goods and tends to discourage maximum production. Whenever aggregate production is reduced at no saving in cost, unit costs rise, intensifying sales resistance, competitive pressure, and the search for more monopolies.

Monopolies can be combatted but not stamped out through legislation. The only way to reduce them permanently is to make them less attractive. If consumer purchasing power equaled the production capacity of the nation, few would trouble to seek monopolies.

International Trade Barriers

Monopolistic practices have their counterpart on international markets. A nation subject to sales resistance and excessive competitive pressure at home may look to foreign markets for unloading its surplus production. It thereby exports competitive pressure to other countries. Foreign governments in self-defense may resort to protective tariffs. Economic conflicts may turn into political conflicts. Eventually a build-up of resentment may lead to military intervention.

International trade barriers restrain international cooperation. They also shelter inefficient domestic firms. The problem can be solved only through recovery of purchasing power and subsequent relaxation of competitive pressure at home. If two or more nations can accomplish this goal within their borders, foreign trade could flourish and international ties could be strengthened.

Stagnation

In summary, the following causes and effects lead to an explanation of stagnation:

1. The use of obsolete management, marketing, and pricing methods.

2. Disregard of the prerequisites for the dependable operation of the price mechanism.

3. Chronic profit-margin distortions.

4. Chronic intermarket supply-and-demand mismatches.

5. Inefficient consumer service.

6. Reduced output.

7. Waste of purchasing power.

8. Increased unit costs.

9. Sales resistance.

10. Need for sales effort.

11. Market uncertainty.

12. Uncertainty of income.

13. Excessive competitive pressure.

14. Pursuit of monopoly.

15. International trade barriers.

16. Stagnation.

From Stagnation to Unemployment

The difference between stagnation and unemployment is only a matter of degree. Stagnation is amplified by macroeconomic factors into mass unemployment. The factors are the so-called Keynesian "independent variables." By calling them independent, Keynes gave notice that he was not interested in investigating the microfoundations of these variables. The factors are the degree of liquidity preference, the size of the money supply, the marginal efficiency of capital, and the marginal propensity to consume. The four variables are neither good nor bad. They are part of the macroeconomic process and are necessary to achieve full employment and prosperity. Their variations depend on the health of the microeconomy. In a nonspeculative economy, the first variable is reduced to zero, and the other three reach their highest levels. Employment is in no way limited or affected. In a modern industrial economy with a tendency toward stagnation, all four variables act in reverse and restrict employment.

Degree of Liquidity Preference

This variable denotes a defensive attitude on the part of the investor. In that respect, it is parallel, on the financial level, to sales resistance on the commodity level. The consumer defends himself, when his purchasing power is eroded and commodity prices are inflated, by resisting unbridled consumption; similarly the investor, who searches for safe and profitable opportunities but finds financial uncertainty in most media, protects his capital by holding some of it in liquid form.

Sales resistance occurs first; it produces market uncertainty, affects business profits, creates financial uncertainty, and thus invites liquidity preference. If sales resistance can be conquered, which will require the recovery of purchasing power now going to waste, it is hoped that market uncertainty will shrink, that business profits will be safe, that financial uncertainty will fade away, and that liquidity preference will vanish.

Size of the Money Supply

At first the money supply may appear as a more or less fixed quantity. But when related to changing needs, the adequacy of money is subject to variations. If the production and distribution process is less than fully efficient, the investment of capital sustaining that process participates in the inefficiency. Additional slices of money are needed. Moreover, when sales resistance dictates a sales effort, the latter requires supplementary financing.

The interest rate, determined by the first two factors, varies directly with the degree of liquidity preference and inversely with the money supply. Distorted profit margins increase the degree of liquidity preference and decrease the adequacy of the money supply. On both counts, the interest rate rises and the level of employment falls.

Marginal Efficiency of Capital

In a nonspeculative economy, the efficiency of capital is sufficient to provide employment for the last increment of manpower. But if there is a ceiling to what can be produced at a profit, the same ceiling limits the efficiency of capital and thereby the level of employment. Together with the first two variables, the marginal efficiency of capital limits the size of investments. Unless investments are adequate, manpower utilization remains below full employment.

Marginal Propensity to Consume

The marginal propensity to consume is the complement of the marginal propensity to save. The propensity to save is made up of two factors: sales resistance due to inflated unit costs and sales resistance due to the uncertainty of income. The consumer, who is unaware of underlying pressures and tensions, considers saving simply as a means of storing resources for future consumption. Together the effective consumer demand and total savings add up to the actual purchasing power but fall short of equaling the production capacity. A slice of potential purchasing power is wasted by the least stimulated firm in each pipeline, which becomes the bottleneck, limiting total output of the pipeline. When all the pipelines are cumulated, the limit is put on the gross national product. This, Keynes did not suspect. The mathematics of his macroeconomic model do not accommodate reclaimable purchasing power.

The marginal propensity to consume varies inversely with the increase in unit costs over and above the economic value of goods. In addition, it is sensitive to the uncertainty of income. The working and investing consumer who must pay prices exceeding the economic value of goods and is, at the same time, exposed to uncertainty of income tends to be selective in his purchases and to lay aside a higher portion of his earnings as a reserve.

Unemployment

All four factors of the Keynesian employment equation are directly influenced by the accuracy of profit-margin equilibration. If inaccurately balanced profit margins simultaneously increase the degree of liquidity preference and lower the effectiveness of the money supply, the marginal productivity of capital, and the marginal propensity to consume, then the level of employment that they determine is limited concurrently from four directions. There can be no question about the potency of such a syndrome.

Keynes presented the four variables primarily as factors limiting employment levels below that of the total labor force. Since he did not trace the causes of the fluctuations of these variables, he could not conceive of them as our most potent allies in ensuring full employment. Should stagnation be brought under control some day, there would be nothing for the four independent variables to amplify, and they would then become instrumental in promoting full employment.

It has been argued that unemployment would be impossible in an ideal, fully competitive economy. The same has been claimed for stagflation. In reality, unemployment would continue even under full competition because monopoly is not its prime cause. Full employment cannot exist in a speculative economy. The claim would have to read: in an ideal, fully competitive, nonspeculative economy, unemployment would be impossible. But, since monopolies would tend to disappear in a nonspeculative economy, unemployment can be said to result, in the last resort, from speculative production in a multistage economy.

From Inefficient Consumer Service to Instability

The explanation of business cycles is quite different from that of unemployment. It starts again where stagnation started, with microeconomic inefficiencies in meeting the consumer demand. The explanation again comprises two stages: from inefficient consumer service to economic instability and from instability to business cycles.

Coexistence of Conflicting Supply Speeds in the Pipeline

Static supply-and-demand disparities, at prices equaling the economic value of goods, are due to changes in demand and/or in costs, as well as to chronic interstage profit-margin distortions. The former is normal and healthy; the latter is not. Random changes in demand and costs depend on function A and function B price adjustments for proper response. Function A of the price mechanism adjusts the demand only: the price moves until the demand accommodates itself to the existing supply. Function B adjusts the supply; the price movement is relayed to all upstream markets so that the supply tends to conform to the demand. Function C is the vertical allocation and equilibration of profit margins.

Function A is always efficient because it involves only one market. Function B, which encompasses several sequential markets, is less than fully effective in a speculative economy. Therefore another function A price movement steps in, obliterating every trace of the remaining disparity. It has caused the demand to yield to the existing supply, but the supply may not have been accurately adjusted to the demand.

Chronic profit-margin distortions at successive stages have a similar effect on static supply-and-demand relationships. There is one significant difference: the effect of chronic distortions is continuous and cumulative. Conflicting dynamic supply-and-demand speeds at prices equaling the economic value of goods, resulting from profit-margin distortions, need not be far apart to build up substantial and growing shortages or excesses. The cumulative effect of small supply-and-demand speed differentials that are incompletely corrected may be serious, especially when the self-adjusting mechanism is prevented from functioning effectively.

An efficient function B adjustment could temporarily bring the straying supply in line with demand, although this may have to be repeated endlessly. Function B, however, may not be reliable. The only effective and permanent response would be provided by repeated adjustments of unimpeded function C. Of the three functions of the price mechanism, function C is the most essential, most delicate of attainment, and most easily impaired. As a result, chronic dynamic supply-and-demand speed conflicts and cumulative static supply-and-demand mismatches are likely to continue on every market.

How can conflicting supply speeds coexist for very long within the same economic pipeline? Inventories provide temporary buffers effective in offsetting improperly matched supply volumes, but inventories are not infinitely flexible. They have an absolute floor below which they cannot be driven. And although they have no absolute ceiling, warehousing facilities may set a constraint. The practical limit is dictated by the cost factor: the cost of storage and the funds frozen in stocks of merchandise.

Substitution of Function A for Function C
Price Movements

Eventually the chronic speed differential due to ineffectual operation of function C of the price mechanism is converted into a succession of function A price movements. Since profit margins remain distorted and the speed differential is perpetuated, it is no longer a matter of a single or a few price movements; it is a situation where an indefinite repetition of fluctuations of the function A variety is prompted, all in the same direction. For months on end, prices inch forward or slip down, without anyone realizing what is going on. This sequence may explain the prime causes of inflation or deflation.

There are a number of reasons why the microeconomic foundations of inflation and deflation have escaped the scrutiny of investigators for so long. The allocation of profit margins to successive firms along marketing channels is not easy to observe. The speed conflict, at prices equaling the economic value of goods, cannot be measured since one of its terms is hypothetical. The static supply-and-demand mismatches, still in terms of a hypothetical value, can be due to any one of a number of reasons. Inventories have a way of expanding and contracting that appears erratic; and even though they are measurable, they are only symptoms. As a result, the continuous inflationary or deflationary price trend remains a mystery.

With rising or falling price trends firmly established, one may ask why these trends do not continue indefinitely but always come to an end. The question can be answered easily but indicates a basic misunderstanding of the problem. The real puzzle is why the trends are not reversed sooner. If instead of climbing or falling for many months, they were reversed once a week, there would be neither inflation nor deflation. These would be effectively checked. Self-adjusting mechanisms, such as the price mechanism, if allowed to operate unimpeded, would be capable of achieving stability.

The reversals of inflationary and deflationary trends at the peak and trough of the business cycle are merely an indication of the finite flexibility of the economy. A point is reached when, under the influence of various constraints, the price mechanism eventually and gradually finds a way to convey desirable signals to the extreme markets. This reverses the engines. A new phase of the cycle has been launched. Because there will be no opposite constraints for many months, the economy engages on a seemingly endless voyage to the opposite pole of the cycle.

Self-adjusting controls are loose instead of tight, leaving the economy to ride on the wings of the winds, instead of steering it firmly toward the responsible discharge of its mission: the efficient fulfillment of consumer wishes, within an atmosphere of prosperity and stability.

The Precession Effect

On each market, function A price movements may erase supply-and-demand speed differentials so promptly that they never materialize in the form of static supply-and-demand mismatches. They are converted directly from conflicting speeds into continuing price movements. That phenomenon may be compared to the precession effect in a gyroscope.

In a gyroscope, forces applied in one plane are deflected into forces acting in a plane at right angles to the first. This happens continually, not after the force has moved the gyroscope in the original plane. As the force is applied, the gyroscope moves instantly in the new direction. The phenomenon, known as the precession effect, describes the initiation of inflation or deflation; the dynamic speed differential between supply and demand, once inventories have absorbed some of the resulting static disparities, is translated directly into a continuing price movement on every market. As a result, no empirical observation or measurement can detect a clue to the phenomenon. The precession effect explains the price behavior that business-cycle theorists have described as a *self-reinforcing, continuous-progression price movement* but for which they had found no motor power.

An Example: Lagging or Leading Output

In a given pipeline, profit margins are allocated to successive firms in unbalanced proportions. The incentive to produce raw materials, for example, is insufficient in relation to the consumer demand for finished goods at prices equaling their economic value. Finished goods cannot be offered to consumers at a faster speed than the rate at which raw materials are extracted without depleting inventories in the pipeline. A scarcity of consumer goods is felt as soon as the pipeline dries up. Retail prices move up. If the price movements were instantly and accurately transmitted back to raw-material producers, these would be induced to speed up their production. But because of the many impediments thrown by ineffective management practices into the path of the price mechanism, retail price rises are not relayed upstream instantly or accurately. When they eventually percolate through to earlier stages, they are likely to be distorted in their proportions; often they are absorbed on the way and fail to reach the raw-material stage altogether.

Such behavior has a double effect: it prolongs inadequate incentives at the raw-material stage and overstimulates those stages closest to the consumer. Therefore the rise in retail prices actually intensifies the inaccurate balance of profit margins at successive stages. The disproportion of profit margins is the basic condition that brought about the original price rises. An increase in the disproportion drives prices higher still. Thus the whirl repeats itself: profit-margin distortions, inadequate stimulation of raw-material production, dynamic supply speed discrepancies, cumulative static supply shortages, repeated retail price rises, and further profit-margin distortions. Thus prices climb the spiraling steps of inflation.

If and when retail price increases finally reach the raw-material stage, the delay alone (assuming the amplitude is accurate) suffices to cancel out the desired effect. If by the time raw-material production is finally stimulated, the speed of the demand has further exceeded the supply rate, the speed differential is perpetuated instead of being canceled. Here is a case where a late adjustment in the speed of the supply does not induce a late speed equalization, but no equalization at all.

This process is repeated over and over for months on end, with all prices advancing continually. Eventually, because various constraints in the economy come to the rescue of the ailing price mechanism, profit margins at the raw-material stage are stimulated enough to begin closing the gap between the speeds of supply and demand. Even when the two speeds are finally synchronized, this only stops the static disparity from getting worse; it does not reduce it. It is necessary for the flow of goods to exceed the speed of the demand in order for the backlog of the static demand to begin melting away. The depleted pipeline is first replenished with adequate inventories. Then supply on the retail market actually catches up with demand. The excessive supply speed must be maintained until an overabundant static supply stops the upward movement of retail prices. The peak of the cycle has now been reached.

The description of deflation is exactly the reverse. Inaccurate vertical equilibration of profit margins results in excessive stimulation at the raw-material stage. Quantities of raw materials produced exceed the consumer demand for goods incorporating them. Retail prices sag. But the signal of falling retail prices does not reach raw-material producers instantly or accurately. Not only are supply-and-demand speeds not synchronized, but profit-margin distortions are accentuated, driving down retail prices, and the process is repeated over and over. By the time the signals to slow production reach raw-material producers, consumption has fallen still further, and the slowing is insufficient; the speed differential remains unchanged. Finally the economic constraints bring about a deceleration both in absolute volume and relative to consumption. The two flows become synchronized; but for bulging inventories to begin receding, the supply speed must fall below the demand speed. Eventually the supply reaching retail markets has been sufficiently discouraged for retail prices to stop falling. The trough of the cycle is at hand.

It is only natural that entrepreneurs and consumers should react to the ebb and flow of business by adapting their activities to the mood of the economy.

Stock Manipulation

Faced with the waves of inflation and deflation, the entrepreneur adapts to them. He finds it both possible and profitable during inflation to stock up with materials, parts, or finished goods beyond the level required by current operations. If he can acquire now at cheaper prices commodities he will need in future months, it is to his advantage to do so. He will derive an additional slice of profit not related to the regular business, a practice advisable in view of the losses he may have to sustain when, during deflation, his inventories tend to lose value.

When the trend is deflationary, it is to the firm's benefit to use up stocks bought at higher prices as soon as possible, before falling prices cut into profits or produce losses. Thus inventory levels will generally fall below the normal needs of the business.

In either case, trading in commodities on the side has an amplifying effect on the established price trend. Inventory manipulation prolongs and intensifies, in the same direction, the supply-and-demand disparities resulting from distorted profit margins. To an inadequate profit margin at the raw-material stage corresponds an insufficient output and rising retail prices; the output is further slowed down at all stages by the acquisition of stocks held for future sale at higher prices, and prices are pushed to still higher levels. Conversely, to an excessive profit margin at the raw-material stage corresponds overproduction and falling retail prices; the output is further accelerated at all stages through the reduction of inventories undertaken to prevent losses, and prices are driven even lower. In both cases the original disparities are aggravated.

Stock manipulation should not be blamed on the entrepreneur. He may not even be aware of his participation. He has no way of knowing whether the original disparities (assuming he can detect them) are not due to a natural cause, such as a change in the demand for certain goods or a shift in production costs. And he has no means of segregating the portion of disparities due to profit-margin distortions from the portion due to natural causes. Even with the required knowledge, he would have no choice in the matter. He either seeks maximum profits and survives, or acts in the interest of stability and exposes himself to business failure.

Inventory manipulation would present no danger and would offer no advantage if profit margins remained undistorted.

Deviations of the Consumer Demand

The consumer is likewise influenced by inflation and deflation. When he is faced with rising prices, without knowing anything about the reasons, he is apt to satisfy some of his needs and wants now rather than having to pay higher prices in the future. When prices are falling, he finds it to his advantage to defer the acquisition of some products for which his requirement is elastic until prices reach lower levels.

Deviations in the consumer demand accentuate, in the same direction, the speed differential between supply and demand and exaggerate price oscillations. When the trend is already inflationary, the increased consumer

demand widens the gap between the inadequate output and swelling requirements; already rising prices are again whipped to higher levels. When prices
are falling, the overabundant supply further exceeds the receding consumer
demand, and prices are further depressed. The result in both cases is a reinforcement of the original disparities.

The so-called psychological factor, to which price fluctuations have
been ascribed by a number of authors, is a reaction of producers and consumers to purely economic stimuli. Once the latter are explained, the mystery
is taken out of the seemingly fickle behavior of firms, consumers, costs, inventories, and prices. That behavior appears surprisingly rational in view of the
distortions of profit margins and the resulting vagaries of the price structure.
Human nature, it is said, is unpredictable; yet it would be much more aston-
ishing if individuals did not respond as they do to the impact of inflationary
and deflationary price trends.

Instability

The following effects summarize the explanation of economic instability:

 1. The use of obsolete management, marketing, and pricing methods.
 2. Disregard of the prerequisites for the dependable operation of the price
    mechanism.
 3. Chronic profit-margin distortions.
 4. Chronic intermarket supply-and-demand mismatches.
 5. Inefficient consumer service.
 6. Coexistence of conflicting supply speeds in the pipeline.
 7. Substitution of function A for function C price movements.
 8. The precession effect.
 9. Lagging or leading output.
10. Stock manipulation.
11. Deviations of the consumer demand.
12. Instability.

From Instability to Business Cycles

Inflation and deflation are the piston strokes that energize cyclical price
fluctuations. The fluctuations might be more tolerable were they not subject

to a number of well-known amplifying elements, long believed to cause business cycles. They should not even be called proximate causes because elimination of the elements would not prevent cyclical fluctuations and their presence is indispensable to the stability of the economy. Thus, amplifying elements are only potential troublemakers; they become troublesome exclusively when profit margins are and remain distorted, and they are actively beneficial and stabilizing when profit margins are properly equilibrated.

Fixed Capital Investments

This is one of the most potent amplifying elements at work in boosting instability into business cycles. In comparison with fluctuations in the consumer demand, fluctuations in capital investments are much more pronounced. The acceleration principle plays an important role in many of the existing business-cycle theories. This principle operates even when the economy is stable. Important changes in the demand or in costs require adjustments in production facilities and equipment that involve large capital expenditures. There is always an element of risk in decisions of such magnitude. But with a stable demand, the problem is manageable.

In an economy characterized by instability, the situation is far different. The consumer demand is possessed of an inflationary or deflationary movement. During the inflationary phase, the demand increases, and the need arises for expanding production and distribution facilities. It appears safe to invest capital into additional plant and equipment inasmuch as the demand is swift and rising. Hence the majority of heavy construction projects are launched during the expansion phase of the cycle. The impact is felt in the already deficient supply line as further depletion and as further postponement of speed synchronization.

During the deflationary phase, the demand contracts, and the expanded facilities are no longer fully utilized. Should liquid funds grow scarce, it may be desirable to sacrifice some of the new facilities for the sake of survival. This adds commodities to already saturated markets, intensifying the downward price movement and prolonging the period of excess supply over demand. Thus, the acceleration principle is like a game of crack-the-whip, in which the leader pulling the chain suddenly stops, and the last ones holding hands are violently propelled forward in a large circle.

When that phenomenon is superimposed on the wide oscillations of economic instability, it invariably tends to reinforce the upward as well as the downward phase. For the sake of stability, investments should be concentrated in periods of contraction, but they never appear justified by the consumer demand. Thus the amplification of inflation and deflation takes place, first, during the period of investment and, later, when surplus facilities are liquidated. The net effect of instability is to add enormously to the uncertainty of long-term investments and to the problems of management. Meanwhile economic instability has been powerfully accentuated.

Interest Rates

Variations in interest rates follow the phases of the cycle, with maximum levels being reached close to the peak and minimum levels near the trough.

If the Keynesian formula is invoked, the interest rate rises with the degree of liquidity preference and falls as the money supply increases. Liquidity preference results from a scarcity of safe and profitable investment opportunities, which characterizes the deflationary phase. The money supply is drained by prices in excess of the economic value of goods, as well as by unproductive sales-promotion activities. The two variables do not exactly coincide in their movements, lending a somewhat blurred oscillation to interest rates. These are rising during most of the expanding phase of the cycle and falling during most of the contraction.

Interest rates have a detrimental influence on the disparities between supply and demand. To an insufficient supply is added a rising interest rate, which slows down business operations and invites a further price rise. An excessive output is followed by a falling interest rate, which encourages business, further depressing prices.

Variations in interest rates act as a beneficial self-adjusting mechanism in a stable economy. They become harmful only under conditions of economic instability.

The Credit Policy

Two elements influence the credit policy: the profitability of investments promotes the extension of credit; the risk of investments inhibits it. The two elements follow closely the sinusoids of the consumer demand. A stable demand would favor a continuing liberal credit policy.

In a situation of instability, the credit policy varies widely. Confidence waxes and wanes following repeated favorable or disappointing experiences; thus the credit policy usually lags behind the real needs of the economy. It is most favorable during the expansion and most restrictive during the contraction of the cycle. This means that it contributes to pushing prices up in inflationary periods and down in deflationary times. The credit policy therefore amplifies instability in both directions.

The Propensity to Save

Saving bears a resemblance to liquidity preference in that it represents an abstinence from utilization—in this case from consumption. Since consumption is essential to a healthy economy, any inclination (justified or not) to restrain consumption may act to reduce the level of employment. This is so whether or not amounts saved are invested.

Savings occur usually during the descending phase of the cycle when the need for reserves looms greatest. The timing is such that fuel is withdrawn at the very moment when the demand is already below the supply. The marginal propensity to save rises, through postponement of purchases the need for which is sufficiently elastic, when prices are falling and unemployment is on the increase. The reverse takes place during periods of rising prices, when dissaving is viewed as safe and consumption as desirable. The speed differential between supply and demand and price fluctuations are further accentuated.

Frequency of Innovations

While the distribution of discoveries and inventions throughout the phases of the cycle is close to random, their commercial exploitation remains tied to the mood of the economy. During inflation, confidence is growing, capital is available, demand is rising, and innovations have their best chance to be successful. Thus they become bunched during expansion regardless of when the basic discoveries or inventions took place. What is significant to the argument is that innovations tend to coincide with periods when prices are on the rise. They whip the galloping demand, and prices are driven higher still.

When deflation sets in and innovations would be particularly welcome, sponsors are hard to find for anything new; the risk is too great. This again, by not stimulating the demand, has a depressing effect on prices.

Employment Levels

Chronic mass unemployment varies in intensity with the four phases of the cycle. It is highest near the trough and lowest near the peak.

Since employment is essential to income and income to consumption, the employment level has a direct influence on the consumer demand. At a time when the demand is leading supply and prices are on the rise, increasing employment adds slices of purchasing power on retail markets, pushing the consumer demand and prices even higher. During deflationary periods, slices of purchasing power are withdrawn from retail markets by workers laid off, reducing by that much the aggregate consumer demand when it has already slipped well below the volume of the supply. Prices are again depressed.

The influence of the level of employment on the health of the economy is so pronounced that it has a feedback effect: for every hundred workers discharged, a certain number of additional workers are likely to lose their employment. During inflation the reverse is true. In both cases, prices are made to fluctuate even more.

Business Cycles

I have divided the description of the process that leads from the inefficient fulfillment of the consumer demand to business cycles into two steps. The first step shows the sequence of events that leads from inefficient consumer service to instability; the second presents a number of well-known amplifying elements that expand instability to the stature of business cycles. Several of these amplifying elements traditionally have been believed to cause business cycles. In reality, their removal would not stop the cycles, and their presence is indispensable to the achievement and maintenance of economic stability. They intensify inflationary and deflationary fluctuations only after these are established by entirely different causes. The succession of factors follows:

1. Fixed capital investments.

2. Interest rates.

3. The credit policy.

4. The propensity to save.

5. The frequency of innovations.

6. Employment levels.

None of the amplifying elements is harmful in itself. All are beneficial to the economy and help maintain stability unless a condition of alternating inflation and deflation preexists as a result of chronic profit-margin distortions and supply-and-demand speed conflicts in the pipeline. Then they exacerbate internal economic maladjustments and amplify the swings in business activity and prices.

The result is full-fleged business cycles. This macroeconomic phenomenon has shaken America a number of times in the past 150 years and has received the attention of innumerable economists. No one has given a convincing explanation of why we must have business cycles. The truth is that we are bringing instability on our own heads through the use of marketing practices truly incompatible with modern production and distribution methods. The prevention of business cycles is predicated on a recognition of that incompatibility.

From Political Excesses to Stagflation

The political roots of stagflation are essentially related to the special privileges granted by the government to certain groups, privileges that reduce the competitiveness of the economy. They are related also to exaggerated fear of unemployment and fear of the spread of communism. The result of these fears has been the unrestrained recourse to the Keynesian receipe and the overextension of the U.S. government in the direction of providing benefits to the masses. Because of a lack of providence for the future, of long-range planning, and of sound public finance, those measures have proven ruinous. They also have invited stagflation.

Stagflation is a vicious situation. Every deficit year that passes increases the fixed debt-service portion of the budget, reducing by that much the chances of future balance. If the federal budget could be balanced, it would take very little more of an annual outlay above interest payments to wipe out the public debt over a period of years. To be precise, if the average interest rate on the public debt is 8 percent, it takes less than 1 percent more per year to amortize the debt over a thirty-year period. It would actually cost 0.88 percent more, for a total of 8.88 percent per year, to repay the entire debt, regardless of its size. This would go a long way toward stopping inflation, letting interest rates come down, stimulating business and employment, and thus escaping from the clutches of stagflation.

5

Theory of Value, Supply and Demand, and Competitive Pressure

A Theory of Value Based on Nonspeculative Production

The profit-motive theory of unemployment and business cycles is an analytical development based on a suspicion, first advanced in 1939, that speculative production may have harmful consequences in a multistage economy. Specifically, it was suspected that speculative production and distribution, by interfering with the free operation of the price mechanism, may make the economic process inefficient. This effect may occur quite independently of the degree of accuracy of expectations and predictions pertaining to the consumer demand in terms of costs and may materialize even if all predictions are correct.

A nonspeculative economy, in which all production and distribution is initiated exclusively after receipt of and in response to a prepaid consumer order, differs fundamentally from a modern, industrial economy. Such a hypothetical economy is, nevertheless, that described by the classics and by Walras, Marshall, and other pre-Keynesian economists, even though they were unaware of it. Their portrayals of economic processes, therefore, were quite unrealistic and provided no assistance in accounting for stagnation or instability. Our speculative and vertically specialized economy was awkwardly recognized by Keynes, who acknowledged chronic unemployment. His model was more realistic but remained unexplained.

If unemployment and business cycles are unknown in a nonspeculative economy and inevitable in a speculative one, then the model of the economy does make a difference, and other factors dissolve into the background. Therefore the standard proposed here for the economic value of goods is *the price at which goods would tend to sell in a nonspeculative economy*. This standard is not the only one that can meet the requirement. Others that could serve equally well are the price at which goods would tend to sell

1. In a single-stage economy.

2. Where all price fluctuations were relayed instantly and accurately to the extreme markets.

3. Where all three functions of the price mechanism were performed efficiently.

4. Under conditions of undistorted profit margins.

5. In an economy where the consumer demand were met efficiently.

6. In a speculative production economy where precautions were taken to ensure the free operation of the price mechanism.
7. Or, more generally (as suggested in Chapter 3), in an efficient, prosperous, and stable economy.

All of these variations reflect the same character of unreality. All are hypothetical. But so is a healthy and efficient economy. All variations are borrowed from a broader, generalized economic system of which our present economy is but a special case. Unless we are imaginative and adventuresome enough to let our minds pierce the ceiling of our confining reality, we will never be free and never make substantial progress. We must supplement empirical research with the necessary analytical thinking, and that thinking must be hypothetical. We must think in terms of a healthy, efficient, non-Euclidean economy to which our reality is related. Only then can we hold out real hope for the future of capitalism amid democratic freedom.

What are the possible applications of the standard of economic value? First, it is indispensable to the analytical reasoning that seeks to develop meaningful cause-and-effect relationships. For example, the links between distorted profit margins, supply-and-demand mismatches, stagnation, and instability could not have been established without the anchor of the standard of economic value.

In addition, two specific applications are measurement of the cross-market supply-and-demand relationship and measurement of the degree of cross-market competitive pressure.

Measurement of the Cross-Market Supply-and-Demand Relationship

The argument in chapter 3 was concerned with static and dynamic, single-market and intermarket, supply-and-demand relationships. For such relationships to carry meaning, price must be specified, but nothing in traditional economic theory is more elusive, indefinite, unstable, and variable than price. There is no standard whereby to judge the economic value of goods. And if price cannot be pegged to a standard, how can the supply-and-demand relationship be gauged?

The supply-and-demand relationship can perhaps be measured if a definition can be found for the concept of supply-and-demand equality. Then static relationships could be categorized into deficient, even, or excessive supply ratios. And if greater precision were needed, the supply could be expressed in percentages of demand, such as 75 percent, 100 percent, or 150 percent.

Dynamic, multistage supply-and-demand flows could likewise be measured by their comparative speeds: lagging, synchronized, or excessive supply speeds. For higher accuracy, supply speeds could be recorded in percentages of demand speeds. The problem is the mathematical definition of the relationship of supply-and-demand equality.

With a standard of economic value, such a definition becomes possible: *Supply-and-demand equality prevails only when goods sell at prices equaling their economic value.* When the definition of the economic value of goods is substituted, equality can be defined as follows: *Supply-and-demand equality prevails only when goods sell at prices at which they would tend to sell in a nonspeculative economy.*

The hypothetical character of the standard of economic value is not objectionable so long as the reasoning remains in the abstract. But the moment such a standard is applied to a pragmatic situation—as, for example, the measurement of a concete supply in terms of the demand—it seems to preclude a realistic result. The answer to that difficulty is simple: the empirical measurement is unnecessary. The reasoning can continue in the abstract. The desired result is the chain of cause-and-effect relationships that link stagnation and unemployment, instability and business cycles, as well as stagflation, to profit-margin distortions and speculative production. Abstract and hypothetical analysis is necessary if we wish to transcend our present less-than-fully-efficient reality and relate it to a potential, broader, generalized economic system that is fully efficient.

The potential broader, generalized economic system is not totally abstract or foreign to reality. It is clearly defined in terms familiar and meaningful to economists and businessmen alike. Nonspeculative production and distribution satisfies the requirements of efficiency. It directly avoids overproduction and underproduction, as well as wrong product mixes; and by maintaining profit margins undistorted, it indirectly eliminates material waste including the waste of purchasing power, market uncertainty, sales resistance, and all the other effects of misleading profit signals. Nonspeculative business operation ensures, if not constant supply-and-demand equality, then at least a continuous tendency toward equality. Goods tend to sell at prices representing their true economic value. The consumer demand is met efficiently.

Although a nonspeculative economy is not to be found in the modern world, production and distribution to order has a concrete and definite meaning. It is practiced daily for a certain portion of producers' and consumer goods. Most consumer services are provided on demand. It is not advocated that all production and distribution henceforth be conducted on a nonspeculative basis, but it is emphasized that it had never been known that speculative production and distribution had anything to do with unemployment and business cycles and that such a realization is a discovery of some significance.

The use of a nonspeculative economic model as a mathematical standard for measuring the economic value of goods, thereby giving meaning to the analysis of supply-and-demand relationships, is novel and powerful. It has permitted the development of a complete unemployment and business-cycle theory that may lead to a quantum jump in the efficiency of capitalism in future generations.

Measurement of the Degree of Cross-Market Competitive Pressure

Another application of the standard of economic value permits the measurement of competition. Competition, in the eyes of Adam Smith and the classical school of economics, is desirable in order to steer selfish businessmen so as best to serve society. Thus competition performs a vital function. But it can also be detrimental. Cutthroat competition benefits no one. In the end, the consumer may pay for it. Bad competition appeared mainly after the onset of the Industrial Revolution as a result of producing in anticipation of the future demand. Today it is no longer sufficient to promote free competition. Because excessive competitive pressure is possible even under free competition, it is necessary to seek, in addition, optimum competitive pressure, which is neutral—neither excessive nor deficient.

It is now possible to state in mathematical terms what neutral competitive pressure means: *Competitive pressure is neutral when supply equals demand at prices equaling the economic value of goods.* By substituting the definition of economic value, the formula becomes: *Competitive pressure is neutral when supply equals the demand at prices at which they would tend to sell in a nonspeculative economy.*

This is a hypothetical definition that does not permit pragmatic application. But empirical measurements are unnecessary. The purpose at hand is to establish accurate cause-and-effect relationships between the supply-and-demand relationship, the degree of competitive pressure, and the quest for monopolistic protection.

Competition is affected by the existence and severity of monopolistic situations. Between undiluted monopoly, where only the limits to the elasticity of the demand provide a price ceiling, and full competition lie the intermediate degrees of imperfect competition. Other factors affecting competition are frictions and rigidities, taxes and tariffs, regulations and controls.

After imperfect competition and external interventions have been removed, the residue comprises the competitive pressure reflecting the cross-market supply-and-demand relationship, superimposed upon the economic entropy. Entropy plays a decisive role in competition and is in need of measurement. A direct effect of distorted profit margins, the economic entropy underlies the stresses specifically associated with economic stagnation and instability.

The problem is to measure vertical competition between buyers and sellers, as determined by variable supply-and-demand relationships; horizontal competition among sellers; and horizontal competition among buyers. Also of interest is the incentive of sellers and that of buyers to transact business. In all measurements, the cross-market pressure or incentive is to be determined. This is an abstract quantity, escaping observation. It is, nevertheless, real.

Here is the technique developed for measuring competitive pressure. It must be understood that on any one market, just as supply and demand become equated as a result of a price movement, so the horizontal competition among sellers and that among buyers become equalized. Both competitions are brought into balance by a price movement. What is to be measured instead on the pattern of the cross-market supply-and-demand relationship is the cross-market competitive pressure.

The measurement comprises two phases. In the first phase, the effective consumer demand is to be determined. The yardstick is the level of the nation's production capacity. In a nonspeculative economy, goods would tend to sell at prices equaling, by definition, their economic value. The consumers' purchasing power would remain intact, at a level equaling the production capacity. Sales resistance would be unknown, and the effective demand would equal the total purchasing power and the production capacity.

But in our less-than-efficient reality, from the total production capacity must be deducted that portion of consumer purchasing power that is wasted through the reduction in consumer goods attributable to the slowest operator in each pipeline. From the remaining purchasing power is then deducted that slice of sales resistance due to unit costs increased over and above the economic value of goods and that slice of sales resistance due to the resulting uncertainty of income. The residue is the effective consumer demand—a constant. In a modern industrial economy, the effective demand may represent, for example, 71 percent of the nation's production capacity.

The second phase begins with the ratio between the cross-market supply-and-demand relationship and the constant percentage just determined. It represents the degree of vertical competition. In a nonspeculative economy, since the effective demand equals the production capacity, the vertical pressure is always equal to the supply-and-demand relationship. In a real economy, because the effective demand is invariably less than 100 percent, the vertical pressure is always higher than the supply-and-demand relationship.

Suppose that the supply-and-demand relationship is set at five different levels, in a geometric progression, such as: 0.50, 0.71, 1.00, 1.41, and 2.00 (representing the supply in proportion to the demand at prices equaling the economic value of goods); the vertical pressure equals these relationships divided by the constant (effective demand as a proportion of the production capacity)—for example, 0.71. Or the relationship can be multiplied by the reciprocal of the constant. In all five cases, the vertical pressure is above the supply-and-demand relationship. It reaches 0.71, 1.00, 1.41, 2.00, and 2.83. The level of pressure that corresponds to supply-and-demand equality is the reciprocal of the constant. It influences both horizontal competitive pressures and both incentives to do business.

Horizontal competition is measured before and after a price movement. Horizontal pressures vary with the vertical pressure, and the reciprocal of the constant, as follows:

$$A = BV \tag{5.1}$$

$$AB = R \tag{5.2}$$

where A stands for the horizontal pressure among sellers, B for the horizontal pressure among buyers, V for the vertical pressure, and R for the reciprocal of the constant ratio of the effective demand to the production capacity. From these two equations can be derived the two horizontal pressures:

$$A = \sqrt{RV} \tag{5.3}$$

$$B = \sqrt{\frac{R}{V}} \tag{5.4}$$

Competitive pressures are those prevailing at prices equaling the economic value of goods. The supply-and-demand relationship does not long remain unequal; a price movement swiftly erases the disparity. Then while the vertical pressure remains constant, all horizontal pressures become equalized at a level equaling the square root of R, the reciprocal of the constant.

Before as after the price movement, the product of the two horizontal pressures always equals R. In a nonspeculative economy, $R = 1$, and the product of all horizontal pressures also equals 1. This means that before the price movement, the pressure among sellers and that among buyers are exact reciprocals, balancing and offsetting one another. After the price movement, all horizontal pressures are neutral; neutral pressures make possible the maximum number of transactions.

In real life, $R > 1$, and the product of all horizontal pressures is always greater than 1. In consequence, the product of both horizontal pressures, before as after the price movement, is excessive. The two horizontal pressures no longer offset one another. After equalization by the price movement, the horizontal pressure among sellers is excessive, but that among buyers is also excessive. Sellers find they cannot sell all their goods at a profit, and buyers realize they cannot obtain all they want at prices they can afford. This acts as a brake on the volume of transactions, and this is why Say's Law is not applicable to a speculative economy.

The incentive of sellers to sell and of buyers to buy is, before as after the price movement, the reciprocal of the corresponding horizontal pressure among sellers and that among buyers.

A more detailed listing of the concepts used in these measurements follows:

a = The nation's production capacity.

b = The portion of the consumer purchasing power that goes to waste because of the reduction in consumer goods attributable to the slowest operator in each pipeline.

c = The residual purchasing power in terms of production capacity.

d = The slice of sales resistance due to the increase in unit costs over and above the economic value of goods.

e = The slice of sales resistance due to the resulting uncertainty of income.

f = The effective consumer demand in terms of the nation's production capacity—a constant.

g = The reciprocal of the constant.

h = The cross-market supply-and-demand relationship.

i = The vertical competitive pressure between sellers and buyers (unaffected by any price movement).

j = The horizontal competitive pressure among sellers, before the price movement.

k = The horizontal pressure among buyers, before the price movement.

l = The horizontal pressure among sellers, after the price movement.

m = The horizontal pressure among buyers, after the price movement.

n = The incentive of sellers to sell, before the price movement.

o = The incentive of buyers to buy, before the price movement.

p = The incentive of sellers to sell, after the price movement.

q = The incentive of buyers to buy, after the price movement.

The equations involved are as follows:

$$a - b = c \tag{5.5}$$

$$c - (d + e) = f \tag{5.6}$$

$$g = \frac{1}{f} \tag{5.7}$$

$$i = gh \tag{5.8}$$

$$j = ik = \frac{gi}{j} = \sqrt{gi} \tag{5.1, 5.3}$$

$$k = \frac{g}{j} = \frac{g}{ik} = \sqrt{\frac{g}{i}} \tag{5.2, 5.4}$$

$$l = m = \sqrt{g} \tag{5.9}$$

$$n = \frac{1}{j} \tag{5.10}$$

$$o = \frac{1}{k} \tag{5.11}$$

$$p = q = \sqrt{f} = \frac{1}{\sqrt{g}} = \frac{1}{l} = \frac{1}{m} \tag{5.12}$$

Table 5-1 summarizes these measurements and relationships. Its concepts are keyed to the above listing and equations.

As long as the effective consumer demand equals the nation's production capacity, the left column of table 5-1 shows that the vertical competitive pressure equals the cross-market supply-and-demand relationship. The product of the two horizontal pressures, as well as that of the two incentives, is always equal to one. For that reason also, after the price movement, the two horizontal pressures, as well as the two incentives, which are equal to the square root of these products, equal 1, whatever the supply-and-demand relationship.

In the right column of table 5-1, which represents the real economy, the situation is far different. The effective demand reaches only 71 percent of the production capacity. This constant affects the vertical pressure, which is multiplied at every step by 1.41, the reciprocal of the constant. It is neutral if the supply equals 71 percent of the demand and excessive whenever the supply exceeds that level. At supply-and-demand equality, the vertical pressure equals the reciprocal of the constant.

The vertical pressure between sellers and buyers determines the horizontal pressure among sellers. Every figure shown in the left column is now multiplied by the reciprocal of the constant. The horizontal pressure among buy-

Table 5-1

Measurement of the Degree of Competitive Pressure

Concept	Nonspeculative Economy					Modern Industrial Economy				
a. Production capacity	100%					100%				
b. Wasted purchasing power	− 0%					− 15%				
c. Residual purchasing power	100%					85%				
d. Sales resistance (costs)	− 0%					− 9%				
e. Sales resistance (uncertainty)	− 0%					− 5%				
f. Effective consumer demand	100%					71%				
g. Reciprocal of effective demand	1.00					1.41				

	Sellers' Market	Supply and Demand Equality		Buyers' Market		Sellers' Market	Supply and Demand Equality		Buyers' Market	
h. Supply and demand relationship	0.50 0.71	1.00		1.41 2.00		0.50 0.71	1.00		1.41 2.00	
i. Vertical competition	0.50 0.71	1.00		1.41 2.00		0.71 1.00	1.41		2.00 2.83	
Horizontal competition Before price movement										
j. Among sellers	0.71 0.84	1.00		1.19 1.41		1.00 1.19	1.41		1.68 2.00	
k. Among buyers	1.41 1.19	1.00		0.84 0.71		1.41 1.19	1.00		0.84 0.71	
After price movement										
l. Among sellers	1.00 1.00	1.00		1.00 1.00		1.19 1.19	1.19		1.19 1.19	
m. Among buyers	1.00 1.00	1.00		1.00 1.00		1.19 1.19	1.19		1.19 1.19	
Incentive Before price movement										
n. Of sellers to sell	1.41 1.19	1.00		0.84 0.71		1.00 0.84	0.71		0.59 0.50	
o. Of buyers to buy	0.71 0.84	1.00		1.19 1.41		0.71 0.84	1.00		1.19 1.41	
After price movement										
p. Of sellers to sell	1.00 1.00	1.00		1.00 1.00		0.84 0.84	0.84		0.84 0.84	
q. Of buyers to buy	1.00 1.00	1.00		1.00 1.00		0.84 0.84	0.84		0.84 0.84	

ers remains unaffected by the effective demand, at levels shown in the left column. After the price movement, pressures are equalized, all new pressures being excessive instead of neutral. They are computed as the square root of the product of the two horizontal pressures before the price movement.

The incentive of sellers to sell, being the reciprocal of the horizontal pressure among sellers, is deficient at most steps. The incentive of buyers to buy remains as in the left column. The price movement equalizes all incentives at a level below the potential incentive.

A few conclusions follow. The left column of the table describes the type of economy (nonspeculative) that the classical school of economists and many neoclassics believed to represent reality. They therefore excluded unemployment and business cycles. They thought that a laissez-faire policy together with free competition would guarantee efficiency throughout the economy.

There would be no waste of materials or purchasing power. The last unit produced would sell at a price equaling its economic value. Resources, including labor, would be fully utilized. Supply-and-demand disparities would be quickly resolved, the resulting equality being stable. Competitive pressures would thereby be brought back to neutral. A maximum volume of transactions would take place. Prosperity and stability would coexist in permanence.

In contrast, the right column of the table illustrates the strains and tensions, unresolved pressures, and eroded incentives that characterize a speculative economy. These are only vaguely perceived, and no one has put his finger on the motor power (distorted profit margins) that sets the entire sequence of disrupting events into motion. The waste of purchasing power and the advent of sales resistance reduce the effective demand to levels below the nation's production capacity; this alone generates vertical competitive pressures above the supply-and-demand ratios.

Horizontal competitive pressures are influenced directly by vertical pressures. Excessive horizontal pressures among sellers are not compensated by correspondingly lower horizontal pressures among buyers, so when the price movement equalizes all horizontal pressures, the resulting residual pressure remains perennially excessive. Horizontal competition is perceived by businessmen as a constant nagging by their competitors who are trying to gain the upper hand in their markets. But all of their competitors feel exactly the same.

Finally, the incentives of sellers to sell are eroded to levels below unity, which are not offset by correspondingly higher incentives of buyers to buy. After the price movement, all incentives are equalized at deficient levels, discouraging otherwise brisk business activity. This slows down the pulse of transactions, leaving substantial increments of resources unused.

The new theory of value has made possible the theoretical measurement of the supply-and-demand relationship and that of various indicators of competitive pressure. The measurements have brought to light the tensions and pressures that exist below the visible surface of business activity. They show how the economy actually functions. The entrepreneur must operate under unfavorable conditions that make his life difficult and less than enjoyable. It is time relief came his way. What opportunities exist for providing relief are described in part II of the book.

But first, chapter 6 presents the logical framework of the profit-motive theory of unemployment and business cycles. That framework provides the basis for a future mathematical representation and dynamic simulation of a modern industrial economy characterized by vertical specialization in combination with speculative production.

6

Algorithm for the Model of a Modern Industrial Economy

A Generalized System of Economic Thought

A nonspeculative economy does not exist. It is a non-Euclidean concept with no counterpart in reality. Nevertheless it can be established as a norm of the kind of economy in which we would all like to live and do business. It can be set up as a frame of reference by comparison with which other economies can be viewed and appraised. Among such other economies may be systems afflicted with various ailments and inefficiencies. These would all be special cases of the norm or frame of reference.

One such special case could be our own, real, Euclidean economy, afflicted with economic stagnation and instability. It can be viewed and appraised by reference to the norm. It becomes clear that the real economy is subordinated to the norm and draws from the norm explanations and understanding, together with a deeper sense of responsibility toward individuals, firms, and the public. It also becomes clear that the norm, or frame of reference, represents a generalized system of economic thought, which transcends the limited scope of past economic investigations or remedies.

A most important consideration, when comparing the special case with the generalized system, is the nature of their relationship: an organic, ingrown, historical, and measurable filiation. There was a time when the present economy was one with the norm. That was the Golden Age of the classics, the age that made Adam Smith and Jean-Baptiste Say release their admirable pronouncements. But the Golden Age did not survive the Industrial Revolution, and today we have a cleavage between the generalized system, or norm, and its derivative—the special case of our inefficient, ailing economy.

Beside the historical filiation, there exists a statistical bridge between the norm and the real economy. That bridge consists of the proportion of the total production of consumer goods that is initiated in anticipation of the future demand. No one in the past has kept that kind of statistics because its utility was not apparent. The proportion of speculative production is a highly tangible measurement that represents the only difference between the norm and reality.

With these two links clearly established, what is now needed is an algorithm designed to model a modern industrial economy as a function of the norm. The proposed algorithm is susceptible of logical as well as mathematical formulation. The logical formulation consists of a chain of tightly woven theorems preceded by suitable premises, such as axioms, postulates, and definitions. The theorems themselves express a sequence of necessary cause-and-effect relationships.

Logical Formulation of the Algorithm

Premises

Axiom I: The most efficient economy would be one whose self-adjusting mechanisms operated dependably, as the classical laissez-faire school of economics hoped.

Axiom II: Industrial economies of the free world, the historic record shows, have not performed their own adjustments in a manner ensuring either consistently high levels of utilization of their resources or economic stability.

Postulate: A nonspeculative economy, in which all production and distribution is initiated exclusively in response to prior consumer orders, is hypothesized as a model of an economy whose self-adjusting mechanisms operate effectively.

Definition I: The standard of economic value is the price at which goods would tend to sell under conditions specified in the postulate.

Definition II: Cross-stage supply-and-demand equality prevails only when goods sell at prices equaling their economic value.

Definition III: The degree of cross-stage competitive pressure is neutral only when cross-stage supply-and-demand equality prevails and when the effective demand equals the nation's production capacity.

Theorem I

Unless specific preventive precautions are taken, speculative production and distribution practiced in a multistage economy interfere with the free operation of the price mechanism. They hinder in particular, the instant and accurate upstream and downstream relay of price fluctuations between the extreme markets.

Theorem II

To the extent that the transmission of price fluctuations through marketing channels is affected by lags and inaccuracies, profit margins fail to be allocated in balanced proportions to successive firms in the pipeline and are distorted from efficient levels.

Theorem III

To the extent that profit margins are distorted, they induce chronic and systematic dynamic interstage speed conflicts and cumulative static disparities between supply and demand, precluding efficient fulfillment of the consumer demand.

Theorem IV

To the extent that consumer service fails to be efficient, economic stagnation and unemployment are inevitable.

Theorem V

To the extent that consumer service fails to be efficient, economic instability and business cycles are inevitable.

The Profit-Motive Law of Unemployment and Business Cycles

The five theorems can be telescoped into a single statement:

> In a modern, industrial, multistage economy, unless specific precautionary measures are taken, speculative production and distribution, by interfering with the free operation of the price mechanism and perturbing the vertical allocation of profit margins, precludes efficient fulfillment of the consumer demand and generates of necessity economic stagnation and instability; the latter are amplified by known factors into unemployment and business cycles.

Mathematical Formulation of the Algorithm

Although the logical formulation of the algorithm can be translated into mathematical expression, I have not attempted such an operation. I do, however, offer certain suggestions as guides to a successful exercise.

To represent the structure of the economy, a succession of stages and markets along vertical marketing channels provides an adequate model. The minimum number of stages that would be adequate without unnecessary duplication is four: the consumer, the merchant, the manufacturer, and the raw-material producer. Three intermediate markets are the retail market, the wholesale market, and the raw-material market. A single representative pipeline suffices for the demonstration.

To represent the pulsating flow of supply and demand through the economic pipeline requires an oscilloscope. This presents a novel challenge to the mathematical economist: developing equations for a constantly moving and changing multistage activity composed of innumerable transactions, continual production and distribution of supply, and relay of fluctuations in the consumer demand and in costs.

Such equations are to represent the activity in a speculative economy, in accordance with model 4 presented in chapter 2, as well as the same activity in a nonspeculative economy defined by model 3.

In the first phase, a rhythm of the flow of supply is established, governed by a given consumer demand and given production and distribution costs. Together demand and costs determine the profit margin, which sets the pace. Comparison between the two models shows identical results.

In the second phase, demand and costs are subjected to random changes around a fixed average. The flow of supply is observed for its response to the changing consumer demand in terms of changing costs. Results are still identical in both models.

The third phase introduces, into model 4 only, the effect of impediments to the free operation of the price mechanism with the ensuing time lags and inaccuracies in the upstream and downstream transmission of price fluctuations. Appropriate equations, representing impediments, lags, and inaccuracies, are fed into the model. The rhythm of flow in model 4 begins to diverge from that in model 3, which is free from impediments. The divergences reflect failure of function B of the price mechanism.

In the fourth phase, the effect is traced of lags and inaccuracies in the transmission of price fluctuations on the allocation of profit margins to successive enterprises. Additional equations represent the allocation process. When the flows in both models are compared, additional divergences are observed. In model 4, profit margins at successive stages register a gradual, and significant, change in proportions. The cross-stage equilibration, or function C of the price mechanism, is disturbed.

In the fifth phase, the effect of profit-margin distortions on the relative multistage speeds of supply and demand is simulated. The observation becomes more subtle because it is necessary to distinguish among the three functions of the price mechanism and their respective efficiencies. Equations are introduced to represent these various factors. Tensions and pressures, as well as confusion, may be noted in model 4. It becomes apparent that the aggregate volume of supply over a period of time falls below the level reached in model 3. Reduced consumer purchasing power, as well as market uncertainty, sets a limit to total sales; increased unit costs create sales resistance. The pace of economic activity slows down as compared with that in model 3. The efficiency with which the consumer demand is met is eroded.

Additional refinements are optional. Equations can be written to represent the entrepreneurs' response to sales resistance in the form of an extra sales effort, sales promotion, advertising, and their additional costs. Furthermore, the quest for monopoly in its various forms, induced by excessive competitive pressure, also levies its social toll through a dwindling volume of business transactions. A close comparison with model 3 may bring to light all of these disturbances. The full development of the fifth phase describes a condition of economic stagnation that is clearly discernible when compared with model 3.

The sixth phase portrays the generation of chronic mass unemployment or underemployment. Additional equations representing the Keynesian so-called "independent variables" are superimposed on model 4 already steeped in stagnation. A new function must be represented: the proportion of actual versus capacity employment. Each equation must relate the proportion of employment to a Keynesian variable as affected by stagnation. The result should be chronically less-than-optimum employment levels.

The seventh phase illustrates the advent of economic instability in model 4, as compared with the stability of model 3. We revert to the fifth phase, which shows the erosion of the efficiency with which the consumer demand is fulfilled. New equations representing incoming and outgoing inventories are introduced at this point. Inventories are not infinitely stretchable. In model 3, inventories remain stable, acting as temporary buffers pending desirable adjustments, which never fail to follow. In model 4, inventories swell or shrink for protracted periods, revealing a shortage or overabundance of supply in the pipeline. If suitable constraints are built into model 4, these will determine the turning points of inflation and deflation. Expansion and contraction are induced by failure of function C to balance profit margins at successive stages, thereby prompting repeated price movements of function A on every market. Inflation or deflation is generated, causing economic instability.

The amplification of instability into business cycles fills phase 8. Equations are written to represent the various amplifying elements, and these are incorporated into the models. In model 3, there is no instability to amplify. In model 4, every new factor intensifies the existing inflation or deflation, giving it the momentum familiar to students of the cycle. If all coefficients are chosen realistically, the end result should approximate the profile of a typical business cycle.

The eight phases provide the specifications for the mathematical expression of the five theorems or logical statement of the algorithm.

This exercise can be extended through the use of further inputs into the two models. It would be valuable to know the effectiveness of preventive measures, described in part II, and designed for application by producers and distributors to increase the efficiency of their operations and simultaneously reduce the incidence of stagnation and instability. Each measure can be represented by an equation that, when fed into model 4, may counteract its inefficient characteristics. The efficacy of each measure can be assessed through comparison with model 3. It may thus become possible to predict the potential benefits of a preventive program.

Part II
Economic Synthesis

In part I, Economic Analysis, the economic structure and activity has been taken apart, to see why it behaves as it does. An examination has been made of the principal levers at work below the surface, and of the hidden forces influencing the malaise of the economy.

Part II is devoted to the reconstruction of the economy. How do we put it back together again so that it will work more smoothly and efficiently? That endeavor is called here Economic Synthesis.

In part II, six chapters describe options open to entrepreneurs for operating rationally rather than struggling in a world of incompatibilities.

In chapter 7 are set forth certain objectives, opportunities, and requirements as guidelines toward the design of a program of efficient management policies.

Chapters 8 and 9 examine two different groups of solutions. The first exploits known modes of operation that have been found safe; the second advocates the use of new management policies especially designed to be sound and efficient in a modern industrial economy.

Chapter 10 reviews a handful of auxiliary policies that have always been considered desirable but rarely, to this day, found practical. When the specific policies described in chapters 8 and 9 have been implemented and have begun to bear fruit, the time will come when these auxiliary policies can be activated with a chance of success. They will then reinforce the beneficial effects of the specific policies.

Chapter 11 briefly discusses the feasible and desirable role of the government in promoting economic prosperity and stability.

Chapter 12 serves to convey to the reader a sense of reality. In it are described the practices actually in use today in the world of business. Case studies have been conducted among industrial and business establishments of different types, and results are presented in abbreviated form. The chapter transcribes a questionnaire designed to elicit pertinent information from volunteering manufacturers or merchants. The gist of the responses is followed by a general comment on opportunities found for improving the efficiency of operations.

7 Theory and Practice

Potential Benefits of Economic Efficiency

If attainable, what can a nonspeculative multistage economy (or its equivalent) mean to producers and consumers? So many changes may occur that the complexion of the business scene could be noticeably transformed. The advent of efficiency could herald a new beginning: every member of the business community and every consumer would stand to benefit.

To the entrepreneur, economic efficiency could mean a liberation from a variety of threats. Liberation from the obligation to equate supply and demand could mean that profit maximization ensures equation and in addition serves the best interests of society. Liberation from the cost of unmatched velocities of the supply in the pipeline could mean substantial savings through the recovery of waste. Some of the reclaimable waste is consumer purchasing power; if that is recovered, Say's Law could again operate. Liberation from sales resistance could permit the entrepreneur to dispense with many forms of sales promotion, including a large portion of advertising expenses, and also to redirect to productive pursuits personnel now assigned to sales efforts. Liberation from excessive competitive pressure could let the entrepreneur befriend his competitors without fear of being spied upon and could relieve him from the urge to seek protection in the form of monopolistic practices. Liberation from the threat of economic stagnation and market saturation could enable the entrepreneur to accelerate his operations to an optimum rhythm. Liberation from economic instability and market uncertainty could enable the entrepreneur to plan his operations with confidence, without constantly having to revise his projections and policies. Liberation from labor's incessant demands and threats of strike could relieve the entrepreneur of many anxieties. Entry into new fields of endeavor could be facilitated. In short, the entrepreneur could take genuine pride in his work, reap the benefits to which he is rightfully entitled, and look forward to security, prosperity, stability, and growth.

To the consumer, it could mean efficient satisfaction of his wants at stable and affordable prices; freedom from constant search for noninflated prices; assurance that prices are in line with true costs; freedom from being forced into consuming and borrowing through fear of inflation; freedom from having to defer normal purchases through fear of deflation and uncertainty; and freedom from a waste of his purchasing power.

To the worker, it could mean freedom from the threat of unemployment; continuity of income from productive work; remuneration in line with work performed; freedom from antagonism with management because profit maximization would coincide with efficient service to the consumer; freedom from the coercion of unionization to obtain pay raises and fringe benefits; satisfaction of maximum collaboration with management for greatest success of the enterprise; freedom from patronizing and condescension on the part of management; feeling of an equal partnership in an endeavor of common interest.

To the financier, it could mean dependable media for investment, higher yields at lower risks, stable values, no financial crises, and a sound currency on international markets. Recessions could be unknown. The extension of credit could be and remain safe.

To the poor and minority groups, it could mean an effective end to discrimination, and opportunities for self-betterment. The poor as a class could disappear, dissolving among those gainfully employed. They would gain pride and self-esteem as they became useful members of society.

To federal and local governments, it could mean that capitalism works. With unemployment and business cycles conquered, the foundations of Marxism could crumble.

A good portion of the welfare programs could become unnecessary; relief, foods stamps, even unemployment benefits could dwindle in importance. The Federal Trade Commission and the Anti-Trust Division of the Justice Department could be reduced to negligible proportions because competition would be neutral and monopolies of scant interest. Taxation could be greatly reduced because the burdens of government would be alleviated, the tax base would be broadened to include a much-expanded work force, and inflation to stimulate the demand would be unnecessary. Many additional benefits could accrue to the government. The currency could exceed its highest value in history. The morale of the population could be at an all-time high.

Such possibilities for the rejuvenation of industry and commerce, as well as of many facets of economic and social life, could be the reward for appropriate changes in business policy. If stagflation is the penalty of speculative production in a multistage economy, it could suffice, in theory, for preventing it, to avoid speculative production and distribution.

So simple a theoretical solution does not seem possible. That is, however, what is declared by the profit-motive theory of unemployment and business cycles.

Both production to order and vertical integration, states the theory, have the potential to eliminate the entropy problem and its ramifications. If applied integrally, these modes of operation, or equivalents, could restore full efficiency in meeting consumer wants, maintain full employment, and preserve economic stability. These objectives could be achieved permanently.

Principles of Economic Efficiency

All laws of nature operate whether we are aware of them or not. The advantage of discovering natural laws lies in the possibility of modifying at will the conditions under which they operate, so that they will work to our advantage rather than to our detriment.

The profit-motive law of unemployment and business cycles is no exception. It says, among other things, that in a multistage economy, speculative production and distribution, by interfering with the free operation of the price mechanism, perturbs the vertical allocation of profit margins. In turn, distorted profit margins induce conflicting speeds in the flow of supply at successive stages, thereby precluding efficiency in filling the consumer demand. So long as the consumer demand is not met efficiently, the theory goes on to say, unemployment and business cycles are inevitable consequences.

Thus a whole chain of harmful effects proceed from a single source: lags and inaccuracies in the transmission of price fluctuations throughout the economic pipeline. From that recognition can be derived two principles of economic efficiency. These spell out the requirements for designing precautions that entrepreneurs may take to prevent the distortion of profit margins. The first principle reads:

> Fluctuations in the consumer demand must be relayed to raw-material producers directly—through the vehicle of consumption units, not replacement units.

As an example, consider a housewife who, purchasing a floor lamp for her living room, selects one that has just been reduced in price by 20 percent. It is not sufficient, according to the principle, for that price fluctuation to be relayed to the wholesaler through a unit produced and distributed in replacement of that bought by the housewife. Instead the fluctuation must be relayed to all upstream firms through the medium of the very unit she has acquired. How this may be accomplished is not indicated by the principle. But it seems clear that if a way can be found to comply with it, the desired end—the balanced allocation of profit margins—could be achieved.

The profit-motive theory provides two clues as to how the first principle can be observed: through vertical integration or through production and distribution to order, this at the entrepreneur's discretion. In both instances, consumer-demand fluctuations are relayed directly to raw-material producers. Thus, what the clues seem to indicate is that models 2 or 3 could achieve the desired aim. Their advantage would be that insofar as they could be applied in real life, the intermarket relay of price fluctuations would meet with no impediments. This would lend to these measures a high degree of effectiveness. Their applicability, however, is limited. A second principle of economic efficiency is broader than the first; it states:

All price fluctuations must be transmitted to the extreme markets instantly and accurately.

The profit-motive theory has pointed out the incompatibility between production and distribution methods in use today on the one hand and marketing procedures on the other. Marketing procedures failed to evolve along with and keep pace with production and distribution methods at the time of the Industrial Revolution. They are far behind today's almost universally utilized practices of vertical specialization and anticipatory production and distribution.

Measures complying with the first principle consist of resolving the incompatibility by reverting to more primitive methods of production and distribution, those used in the Golden Age. Measures designed to observe the second principle have for their purpose to resolve the incompatibility by bringing antiquated marketing methods up to date with modern production and distribution practices.

Instead of capitulating, the entrepreneur now gives free rein to his imagination, designing fresh ways to market commodities produced and distributed according to the most modern practices. The advantage of developing new marketing techniques is indisputable. It represents progress, an advance toward permanent prosperity and stability without constraints on how goods must be produced or distributed. Up-to-date marketing procedures are applicable to almost any commodities, a much broader spectrum than those admitting of primitive production and distribution measures.

Perhaps, when first applied to concrete situations, the redesigned marketing procedures may require somewhat greater caution. For that reason, it is recommended that all possible approaches be considered and the most effective mix in terms of cost and trouble be adopted. The return to models 2 and 3 should yield positive results; the application of revamped marketing techniques should permit handling a wide variety of goods.

Models Complying with the First Principle

Models 2 and 3 are safe for application to any commodities that lend themselves to rather primitive handling. Both comply with the first principle. They should effectively prevent unemployment, business cycles, and in conjunction with political reform, stagflation.

Model 2

This model consists of horizontal specialization only, combined with anticipatory production and distribution. A single market brings together raw-material producers (who also act as manufacturers) and consumers. Awkward as such an economy may seem, there may well have been a stage in the development of certain economies that corresponded to that model. For that reason, it appears more realistic than model 3. Inasmuch as a return to model 2 could radically eliminate the problems with which we are concerned, it is worthwhile to investigate all of its angles.

Horizontal specialization means the division of labor into parallel and simultaneous production-distribution operations performed by independent enterprises, to the exclusion of vertical specialization. In model 2, vertical specialization, or the division of labor into successive production or distribution operations by independent agents, is absent. Instead the economy is characterized by vertical integration.

Since a total return to vertical integration is out of the question, it may be well to investigate opportunities for partial applications. For example, vertical integration could be applied to certain groups of products, or consecutive stages between the production of raw materials and the consumption of consumer goods could be reduced in number. Whether this is accomplished through vertical mergers, through combinations of successive divisions within a single enterprise, or through the incorporation by a firm of functions formerly performed by suppliers or clients, all of these measures go in the direction of vertical integration and are worthy of consideration.

Model 3

Here horizontal specialization is supplemented by vertical specialization, but production and distribution are nonspeculative. There are no markets and no ready stocks of supplies, only order-taking agents. All stages operate exclusively upon the receipt of advance and firm consumer orders. Such an arrangement is unrealistic, however; it is most unlikely that examples of model 3 have ever existed in its pure form.

Model 3 nevertheless would be extremely effective in preventing the whole sequence of untoward phenomena under study, which makes it worthwhile to study it in detail. Perhaps if total elimination of speculative production and distribution is ruled out from the start, partial elimination might be possible. Production and distribution to order might be applied to certain groups of products or at certain stages. Having not been acknowledged as possessing special merit, that mode of operation has not received any particular consideration nor has it been exploited in the past.

Policies Complying with the Second Principle

Now twentieth-century production and distribution modalities are accepted as a fact of life, and it is the turn of marketing practices to be subjected to a process of modernization and adaptation with a view to resolving present incompatibilities. No longer constrained to reject progress in producing and distributing, the entrepreneur is now challenged to devise advanced marketing techniques fit for use in a modern industrial economy. Imaginative solutions are invited so long as they remain practical and economical.

The Replacement-Pricing Policy

The object is to devise modern equivalents of vertical integration or production to order. Production and distribution for replacement fulfills that mandate. It consists of reordering at frequent intervals those quantities sold to clients and basing the selling price on replacement costs. The procedure, which can be designated *replacement pricing,* may be applied between any two contiguous stages. For best results, it should be repeated at every stage, from retailers to raw-material producers. When that is achieved, the effect is equivalent to that of production and distribution to order, from the standpoint of the dependable relay of price fluctuations throughout the economic pipeline. The provisions of the second principle are observed. Interferences with the balanced allocation of profit margins to successive stages are removed.

The Synchronized-Pricing Policy

Here the instant and accurate transmission of price fluctuations is induced artificially; buyers and sellers take into account current price changes on the extreme and all intermediate markets. The technique calls for frequent reordering of goods sold and comprises means for synchronizing price changes at all stages. Although accomplished artificially, the synchronization of price changes has the same effect: profit margins can remain undistorted.

The Open-Price Ordering Policy

Synchronized pricing involves a modification of the rhythm of reordering. Reorders are to be placed more or less parallel with sales. This could mean more frequent ordering. An increase in the frequency of reordering entails a decrease in the size of each purchase order. The open-price ordering policy is designed to handle the modified ordering procedure without losing the advantage of volume discounts.

For products that do not lend themselves readily to the restrictions of vertical integration or production to order, the techniques complying with the second principle should resolve the problem in a manner that conforms to our times. Their applicability is unlimited.

The approaches identified here should be instrumental in restoring undistorted profit margins and the efficient fulfillment of the consumer demand, thereby also promoting full employment and economic stability.

8 Efficient Economic Models

Models 1, 2, and 3 are safe and sound, efficient and stable. Regardless of external impacts, the price mechanism, which is the main self-adjusting lever of the economy, can perform its three functions to perfection. There are no lags, no inaccuracies, no waste, no sales resistance, no stagnation, no instability.

Model 1, featuring horizontal specialization only with no speculative production, is safe but so primitive that it has no appeal to modern industry and commerce; besides, it is not necessary. Models 2 and 3 are closer to present structures and production modalities. Either is adequate in the way of protection. Under either, the price mechanism can operate dependably, and desirable adjustments can take place without hindrance. The consumer demand is met efficiently, employment is high, and stability is permanent.

Model 4 is realistic. It simulates the industrial economies of the modern world; it features speculative production in a multistage economy. But it is neither efficient, safe, nor sound, and gives rise to waste, stagnation, and instability. What are the possibilities of reverting to models 2 or 3?

The Vertically Integrated Model

This is model 2, still confined to horizontal specialization but evolved to include speculative production and distribution. It is not totally unrealistic; it probably existed at a period preceding the Industrial Revolution, perhaps not in its purest form but approximately. It may be a fair representation of conditions that prevailed during the Golden Age when Say's Law was still valid. Model 2 is safe, sound, and efficient. For that reason, we should examine what opportunities are open to the entrepreneur for taking refuge from the many hazards of doing business within the comparative security provided by that model.

Vertical integration, the opposite of vertical specialization, can be defined as the coordinated performance of successive operations, otherwise commonly executed by separate enterprises, under the authority of a single management. There are many examples of such combinations. A manufacturer may produce some or all of the raw materials he needs; he may sell his output directly to the consuming public; a retailer may produce some of the goods he sells. Many ramifications exist, and they are subject to many alternatives.

A modern industrial economy, in which every entrepreneur performs the functions of producer of the raw materials he utilizes, of mill operator, parts manufacturer, assembler, wholesaler, and retailer of all of his output, is inconceivable. Raw materials can be extracted only where the ground has been blessed by nature, grown only where climate and soil are favorable. Finished products are consumed mostly in urban centers, sometimes thousands of miles distant. Also, manufacturers use many raw materials in moderate quantities, making self-production uneconomical. Finally, the management would be forced to develop adequate competence in many, often unrelated, fields.

The trend has been definitely toward vertical specialization, which can probably be considered an index of the degree of civilization. To reverse the trend entails prohibitive costs, besides being impractical. Nevertheless, it has not been known that vertical specialization, and it alone, may explain the whole chain of modern economic ills. If this is so, it means that the sequence can be stopped in its tracks merely by reverting to vertical integration. That knowledge, if properly utilized, may open new vistas on the potentialities of modern economic life. By upholding vertical integration as a desirable goal, at least in theory, the entrepreneur can perhaps develop some beneficial procedures, even if the goal is only partially reached.

Vertical Integration for Certain Products

Certain groups of products are handled today in a vertically integrated manner, and there may be borderline cases where the newly developed knowledge can provide helpful guidance. For example, the utilities are almost entirely integrated. The big oil companies, coal miners, natural-gas producers, and other enterprises whose output is essentially a single, highly specialized product often involve but one or two stages. The dairy industry is another example.

In small, countryside industry, instances abound. The manufacture of pottery and bricks, the exploitation of a stone quarry or a gravel or sand pit, and truck farming are prime examples of integrated industries. Here the producer frequently delivers the merchandise directly to the consumer.

Where restricted to a single product or line of products, vertical integration gives rise to a nonnegligible volume of practical and economical applications. It may be possible to expand that proportion without undue sacrifice. Where the product lends itself and conditions are otherwise favorable, vertical integration in the production and distribution of certain products appears advisable as a means of preventing the distortion of profit margins.

Vertical Integration at Certain Stages

There are many examples where two pipelines connecting the same raw materials and the same finished goods encompass a different number of stages.

One route is more integrated vertically than another. Some firms perform more successive operations than others.

The term *vertical integration* strictly used applies only where all of the steps from raw-material production to retail sale are performed by a single entity. Yet more numerous opportunities exist for partial integration, at certain stages only. Whenever a single organization can perform the functions of two consecutive firms without complicating operations or increasing costs, a merger of these firms may be considered. The combination may involve two producers, two distributors, or one operator of each type. Occasionally the merger may extend to three or more stages.

The simple merger of consecutive firms does not necessarily guarantee the instant and accurate transmission of price changes up and down marketing channels. Some large companies, such as General Motors Corporation or U.S. Steel Company, are internally organized into autonomous divisions, each of which sells to or buys from other divisions whenever the price is right. Each division keeps separate accounts and is expected to earn a profit for the mother company. From the standpoint of the allocation of profit margins, the legal unity is not sufficient to ensure accurate equilibration. Each division constitutes an independent enterprise, specialized horizontally or vertically. When the specialization is vertical, the problem is identical to that confronting independent firms. It becomes necessary to integrate the company's divisions. If some other approaches described in this chapter or the next can be applied, the vertical structure ceases to be relevant.

Functional Vertical Integration, and Automation

The legal merger of two successive firms is not the only method of promoting vertical integration. Less cumbersome procedures yield the same advantages. One firm may simply add to its established operations some of the functions formerly performed by its suppliers or clients. Such combinations require only the acquisition of the necessary machinery and equipment, as well as qualified manpower.

Certain industries are more fluid than others. In the electronics industry, some firms manufacturing printed circuits also make a number of the components of such circuits. The process can be gradual so that pipelines are forever flexible and interchangeable. Once it is known that vertical integration is to be preferred over vertical specialization, steps can be taken to promote it.

One notable development in this respect is the increasing trend toward automation, sometimes called the second industrial revolution. Its effect on the efficiency of the economy is the reverse of that of the first Industrial Revolution. Early power-driven machinery could perform quickly and cheaply a single operation at a time. This led to higher vertical specialization. Automation consists of linking together a succession of hitherto separate operations. It tends to reduce the number of stages.

Some automation simply consists of doing mechanically operations formerly performed by hand within the same firm. Packaging and handling may thus become automated. But the automation movement distinguishes itself from mere mechanization by combining within the enterprise a succession of separate operations into one continuous process. That trend induces manufacturers to encroach more and more upon the fields of their suppliers and clients until many consumer goods are produced from raw materials in a single run. The contact with the human hand is minimized. Vertical integration is promoted.

Prior to deciding on a course of action, the entrepreneur can make a survey of the number of stages needed for each of his main products. If for any of them the industry as a whole uses fewer stages, he may wish to look into the possibility of imitating the majority. This should be practical and economical. In an effort to reduce the number of stages, he can negotiate with suppliers or clients; in case of opposition, he can switch channels.

To summarize, the management may wish to keep in mind the following possibilities of promoting vertical integration:

1. Vertical integration for certain products.

2. Vertical integration at certain stages.

3. Legal mergers of consecutive firms.

4. Intracompany vertical integration.

5. Functional vertical integration.

6. Automation.

The Nonspeculative Model

Because of the limitations to vertical integration, it is well to consider other approaches capable of meeting the same goal: the uninhibited operation of the price mechanism. The profit-motive theory has given us two clues: vertical integration and production to order. Either, if fully implemented, would suffice. But we know already that full implementation is precluded. For that reason, a simultaneous attack on all fronts is the correct strategy.

Production to order has over vertical integration the advantage of solving simultaneously two problems: the problem of attaining economic efficiency and that of predicting correctly the future demand in terms of costs. Nonspeculative production and distribution ensures that supply and demand are, at all times, either equated, or in the process of being equated, dynamically and statically; it also assures that profits are maximized.

Vertical specialization with production to order corresponds to model 3. It has had rare, if any, pure embodiments in real life. Nonspeculative production is easier to conceive in a single-stage rather than a multistage economy, but that takes us back to model 1. Model 3 is a hypothetical concept, extremely useful for abstract reasoning. It would be highly desirable if it could be implemented. Consider, however, what would be involved.

Leaving out those who work for themselves and those who sell services, every entrepreneur initiates production and/or distribution exclusively in response to firm orders from ultimate consumers. There are no stocks on hand, nor is there need for any markets. There are catalogues, but no set prices. Every order begins with an inquiry about costs and an offer of a price, either of which may be accepted or declined. Even the coal and iron for the nails of a pair of shoes are mined only after receipt of a purchase order, which has been duly negotiated. Clearly the complications of doing business and meeting the needs of everyday living would be staggering. Yet that is what the theory leads us to believe would be a safe system of producing and distributing, in which the demand would never run dry.

Since total production and distribution to order is excluded, perhaps partial operation to order, for certain products only or at certain stages only, may provide interesting possibilities. In fact, such possibilities are much more diverse than those of vertical integration.

Production to Order for Certain Products

Few examples can be found of true production to order for goods involving several stages. Certain building materials, such as stone, sand, and gravel, are extracted to the order of the consumer and delivered to his premises. But no vertical specialization is involved here, and we are back to model 1. Two stages may occasionally be included, as in the case of the sculptor of funeral memorials. After being commissioned to create the monument, he orders a block of granite of suitable size and shape from the quarry. The quarry cuts it after receipt of his order. This is true production to order, provided the sculptor finds out the price of the particular block and takes this into account in quoting to his client the cost of the monument.

It appears doubtful whether many more products are actually produced from the ground up to the order of an ultimate consumer. Many goods are custom-made, but usually the raw materials and many parts are withdrawn from stock. It is not clear how this method of production can very well be expanded. Fortunately other options may be more attractive.

Production to Order at Certain Stages

Production or procurement to order between consecutive stages is common in industry and commerce. Between two distributors—the retailer and wholesaler, for example—the procurement of specialized goods not habitually carried by the retailer, to the consumer's order, is a frequent occurrence. Retailers in small towns cannot afford to carry a full stock of merchandise because the volume of their business does not warrant it. They act as agents for centrally located wholesalers, which stock many more items.

Between a distributor and a producer, there exist many instances where an item is made to order for delivery through a retailer. The retailer receives a firm order from the consumer and then places an order with the manufacturer. The latter makes up the desired item and ships it to the retailer. This process occurs whenever the merchandise is to be personalized, made to measure, upholstered with material selected by the consumer, or otherwise custom-made; it may also occur when goods are special ordered.

Between two consecutive producers, production to order is extremely common. Many manufacturers require custom-made commodities. In the heavy-metals industry, a substantial proportion of forms and shapes are produced only to order. For example, many steel beams for the construction of buildings and bridges, railroad tracks, steel bars for reinforcing concrete, columns, metal pipes, steel plate, etc., are made to engineering specifications. With the exception of standard sizes produced for stock because of a steady demand, metallurgical mills produce a quantity of products to order. Sawmills produce to order beams, studs, boards, moldings, and so forth in accordance with architects' and builders' drawings. Only standard-sized boards and other wood products are made in advance for stock.

So long is the list of custom-made producers' goods that the entrepreneur must frequently have the choice between anticipatory production and production to order. Since he had not been alerted to the soundness of the latter practice, he has had no incentive to give it preference. The profit-motive theory states that by avoiding speculative production, the entrepreneur removes the impediments to the dependable operation of the price mechanism and promotes the balanced allocation of profit margins to successive firms. By the same token, he eliminates errors of judgment in anticipating the future demand in terms of costs, and with them the problem of maximizing profits.

Whether production to order is promoted between two distribution stages, two production stages, or one of each type, it acts to reduce the aggregate volume of speculative production and distribution. If it is kept in mind that unemployment, business cycles, and even stagflation could probably all be eradicated by converting model 4 into model 3, it appears worth the effort to reduce speculative production by all possible means.

Not all products of all firms can be produced and/or procured to order, and for that reason, additional alternatives must be provided to the entrepreneur. One such alternative is a service not now available to the consumer: the advance-order service.

The Advance-Order Service

Both vertical integration and production to order are necessarily restrictive measures. They go counter to the general trend of modern economic activity, which is highly specialized, vertically, and as speculative as possible, thereby facilitating off-the-shelf consumer service. Nevertheless, because of its fundamental soundness and advantage, production and distribution to order should be exploited in all its opportunities. For certain categories of products, it can actually give rise to a new procedure apt to benefit both producers and consumers.

The advance-order service provides to the consumer an opportunity for economical purchasing not now available to him. He must be in a position to foresee his needs and order for future delivery.

The service is operated by the retailer on a volunteer basis. Everyone acts strictly in his own interest. The retailer enters an agreement with certain manufacturers according to which these will produce a portion of their output of selected products strictly to order, procuring the necessary materials and parts only in response to incoming orders. Similar agreements are concluded between manufacturers and their principal suppliers, all the way back to the raw materials.

The waste inherent in chronic disparities between supply and demand is recovered, and the risk involved in anticipatory production is eliminated. The resulting savings can be shared with the consumer whose strained purchasing power is expanded. The price is always up to date, reflecting the current demand in terms of present production costs. Payment can be made at the time an order is written, or it can be placed in escrow in a bank for release on receipt of the merchandise if it conforms to the specifications.

The consumer plans some of his purchases in advance. For example, a young couple may know they will need furniture nine months hence. They visit a dealer, inspect the displays, and select the sets and pieces they like. The salesman quotes two prices—one for immediate delivery and a lower price for delivery eight months later. If this fits in with their plans, they take advantage of the advance-order service.

Because the purpose of the service is to ensure the instant and accurate transmission of price fluctuations, price determination is of the essence. The price that covers production and distribution costs, including profit, is known to the retailer when he receives an advance order, through his suppliers, and their suppliers. Each supplier keeps his clients informed of price fluctuations at every stage. The dissemination of price lists, a practice well established in business, serves that purpose. Price lists, which can be replaced by computer runs, usually remain in effect until replaced. Where orders are frequent, there is no difficulty.

Where orders are far between, the retailer contacts his suppliers, and his suppliers their sources, until raw-material producers are reached. Thus the retailer is in a position to quote a valid future delivery price to the consumer. The procedure is slow. Or the consumer can bid a price; the order is then conditional, subject to confirmation.

Production and distribution to order takes place concurrently with regular (speculative) operations of the participating firms. The physical flow of goods remains undisturbed; only accounts are kept separate, so that certain elements of cost (risk) and profit (uncertainty) can be omitted.

The advance-order service affords a degree of efficiency and safety unknown in present commercial transactions. For example, everyone knows that a new article, such as an automobile, loses value as soon as the first owner takes possession. That loss is due not so much to a decrease in the usefulness of the merchandise as to the high cost of selling it because consumer purchasing power has been eroded. The consumer is made to pay higher prices for overabundant goods because promotional efforts are required to make sales. While the high cost of selling adds no value to the article, the buyer must nevertheless pay for it. That is the slice of the cost which the participating entrepreneur can hope to recover through the advance-order service. For goods so handled, a full measure of consumer purchasing power is reinstated, and the extra sales effort can be dispensed with. Thus the merchandise does not lose value immediately upon being delivered in the same proportion as it often does today. The selling price represents more accurately its intrinsic value, reducing correspondingly the danger of depreciation.

A maximum of flexibility is conferred upon transactions. Whereas usually a return and refund guarantee is costly to the seller, it costs him nothing with the advance-order service. The returned unit is simply allocated to the next client on the list of advance orders; if no subsequent order has been received, the unit is allocated to the regular stock, and the merchant who procured it at a lower cost derives a higher profit.

Installment buying is made safer. Because the merchandise is not subject to high depreciation after delivery, it is sound to extend credit up to a higher proportion of the selling price. The down payment can be omitted. Financing charges can be extremely low. The first installment can be made when the order is placed. Unless installments extend over a period exceeding twice the delivery period, the interest, which is negative until delivery, can be totally eliminated. The residual cost of financing is low because the risk is low. No risk is incurred during the production period. After delivery, the remaining risk is reduced in two ways: payments made before delivery act as a cushion against losses from default after delivery, and the retention by the merchandise of its value after delivery (with the exception of a minute depreciation based on the article's decreasing usefulness) is a second guarantee in case of forced repossession.

The advance-order service has two main advantages: it eliminates cross-stage supply-and-demand disparities at prices equaling the economic value of goods, and concurrently it avoids the risk of errors of judgment in predicting quantities demanded. A slice of consumer purchasing power now going to waste is recuperated. Market uncertainty is diminished. Sales resistance is avoided.

To the extent that the advance-order service can be applied, the merchant can simplify certain functions: there is no warehousing, little displaying, little advertising, no sales promotion, direct home delivery. The service reduces the task of the retailer to that of an order-taking agent.

The advance-order service constitutes for certain products the business procedure par excellence. To the category of custom-made articles (clothing, shoes, eye-glasses), which lend themselves to marketing by that technique, may be added some durable goods, such as furniture and household appliances, certain tools, and so on. Mail-order houses may feature the service.

Since the advance-order service can be applied only to a limited selection of products, results can only be partial. That is no reason for not instituting the service. One slice of consumer goods can be ordered in advance, while another is acquired by other, more appropriate and more widely applicable, techniques.

9 Management Policies Designed for Use in a Speculative Multistage Economy

Modern economic ills may be avoided through vertical integration or production to order. These policies are applicable for certain products or at certain stages and should be utilized whenever otherwise practical and economical. The advance-order service, which spans all stages, holds special merit for those products that permit advance planning of purchases.

Nevertheless, each of these precautions contains a restrictive element. The advance-order service in particular requires of the consumer advance recognition of future needs, initiative in placing orders months ahead, the disbursement of time payments, and willingness to face a protracted waiting period. The entrepreneur also suffers certain inconveniences, such as special ordering and dual bookkeeping. The great majority of retail purchases therefore must continue to be transacted on the spot and require methods more in keeping with the demands of modern production, distribution, and consumption and applicable to a wide spectrum of products.

The object of the procedures described in this chapter is to resolve the incompatibility between production and marketing methods, not by reverting to more primitive ways of producing and distributing but by redesigning marketing methods. Present marketing practices have long been inadequate for use in a modern industrial economy and are in need of being brought up to date.

The techniques presented here are not suggested by the profit-motive theory and no longer comply with the first principle of economic efficiency. The second principle, more liberal than the first, states that all price fluctuations must be transmitted to the extreme markets instantly and accurately. That requirement can be met through the application of three new marketing methods: the replacement-pricing policy, the synchronized-pricing policy, and the open-price ordering policy.

The Replacement-Pricing Policy

For purposes of clarity, this measure is described under two headings: the simple method, which is quite restricted, and the compound method, which has wide applicability.

Simple Method

The replacement-pricing policy, simple method, is an extension of the advance-order service. Suppose a consumer wants to buy a table. The salesman quotes him an immediate delivery price of $100 and a five-month delivery price of $80. The client would like to take advantage of the advance-order service but cannot wait. The salesman then makes him a proposition: he will loan to the customer a unit from his stock, meanwhile ordering one for him. He will charge $5 for the loan. When the ordered unit arrives five months hence, there is no point in making the exchange since both units are identical.

What has been accomplished? The consumer has taken immediate delivery, as is customary today. In fact, he does not even have to know what goes on behind the scenes; all the customer notices is that his dollar goes further. Meanwhile the price which he has paid is not the price of the unit he receives, but that of the unit ordered by the dealer through the advance-order service. In this manner, the latest retail-price fluctuations are relayed to raw-material producers instantly and accurately.

The physical flow of goods between retailer and consumer is identical to that of a speculative transaction, but the pricing has been divorced from it. Without even being aware of it, the consumer pays for a unit ordered in replacement of the unit he receives—hence the designation *replacement pricing*. This is one way to avoid impediments to the free operation of the price mechanism.

To summarize, the replacement-pricing policy, simple method, consists of delivering the merchandise to the consumer without bringing to his attention that it is borrowed from the retailer's stock. The consumer never plans a purchase; at the time of the sale, the merchant orders through the advance-order service a unit in replacement of that "loaned out." The cost of this order becomes the basis for figuring the selling price, which thus equals the replacement price. When the unit ordered is received by the retailer, the exchange is superfluous and therefore omitted.

Through frequently revised price lists, the retailer is informed at all times of replacement costs. These reflect the consumer demand, which fluctuates with the selling price. The same remark applies to all stages preceding the retailer. This should permit the retailer to mark his merchandise with replacement prices and to revise these as the demand or costs change. The selling price incorporates the cost of "borrowing" the unit for a period corresponding to the delivery time.

Stock levels to be carried by the retailer are computed on the basis of average delivery times required by the advance-order service and the average volume of consumer purchases. The technique applies best to merchandise with continuous production, constant demand, and comparatively short delivery time. All of the specifications and advantages of the advance-order service apply to the retailer.

Compound Method

Replacement pricing is an important step forward over the advance-order service, but the simple method is limited in its application on two accounts: it has for the retailer the disadvantage of freezing in inventories a capital vastly in excess of that required to finance customary stock levels. It creates a warehousing problem and involves extra costs. Moreover, the simple method goes counter to the principle of continuity in the flow of merchandise. Goods accumulating in retail warehouses tend to spoil and depreciate. Also, dual accounting is cumbersome. For all these reasons, a further improvement is desirable. The compound method of replacement pricing provides the needed solution.

The compound method preserves the peculiar relationship that exists in the simple method between the consumer and retailer but deletes the use of the advance-order service by the retailer and prior stages altogether. Instead the peculiar relationship is repeated between the retailer and his suppliers, between his suppliers and their suppliers, all the way back to raw-material producers. Between each pair of consecutive stages, all trades are made at the replacement price. Suppliers deliver units ordered in replacement of those sold, under the guise of "loaning" them out. They simultaneously order or put into production a corresponding number of units in replacement of those "borrowed." Exchanges of identical units after delivery, being superfluous, are canceled. Frequently revised price lists, responding to fluctuations in the consumer demand as well as to cost changes, are mailed to regular clients. Suppliers determine minimum stock levels required to satisfy the demands of their clientele.

Because selling costs are low, the merchandise, once sold, retains most of its value, and a satisfaction or money-back guarantee is neither risky nor costly. Down payments can be omitted. A first installment is collected at the time of delivery. The amortization schedule is computed so as to exceed the rate of depreciation. When risk is thus minimized, interest is practically the only cost the consumer assumes. It represents, in effect, the cost of "borrowing" the unit until replaced. The replacement-pricing policy, compound method, combines the advantages of speculative production and distribution for the consumer with those of production and distribution to order for protecting the free play of the price mechanism.

Consider an example. Mr. Brown wishes to present a table clock with Westminster chimes to his wife. He compares clocks on display in several stores, and makes his selection. The retailer has a currently valid price list that gives the latest wholesale price, on the basis of which the retailer computes the retail price. It will be $120. If Mr. Brown accepts that price, he may wish to charge the purchase and make monthly payments. The clock is delivered to his home. The following Monday, for example, the retailer places an order for an identical clock. The order specifies the minimum number of such clocks to be shipped at one time. The manufacturer files the order until he has received a sufficient number of orders to make shipment economical. The physical flow of merchandise is maintained as it is today. Only the pricing is modified.

When using the replacement-pricing policy, compound method, the retailer assumes a risk only with regard to his opening inventory. All subsequent commitments concern merchandise that has been sold before it is bought, involving no risk whatsoever. Except to close it out, there would be no point in selling a unit that cannot be replaced at a lower cost. The simultaneous sale and purchase combination allows the entrepreneur to hedge 100 percent against price fluctuations. Besides the method is efficacious in counteracting and preventing price fluctuations.

Upon receiving orders totaling the number specified by the retailer, the manufacturer ships the clocks. Meanwhile, every Tuesday, for example, he orders the principal parts and materials required to assemble as many units of the clock as have been ordered from him during the past week. When he has received enough orders from his clientele, the manufacturer initiates a run for assembling the clocks.

Parts and material producers in turn adopt a similar policy. Weekly reorders, on Wednesdays for example, combine all the orders received during the past several days from all assemblers. The technique applies also to raw-material producers. No one is unduly inconvenienced.

Minor adaptations are required for handling smaller and less expensive items. The weekly (or perhaps biweekly) rhythm can be maintained, regardless of the unit price. Experimentation will dictate the optimum modalities.

The recommended price-dissemination, ordering, and accounting procedure lends itself ideally to automation. One of the most useful applications of the computer to business may be to assist in implementing the replacement-pricing policy. There seems to be a wide-open field for such applications on a broad scale.

A special benefit of replacement pricing is that market uncertainty, as well as risk, is almost completely averted. On one hand, the price mechanism is permitted to perform its important functions dependably, reducing market uncertainty caused by profit-margin distortions and supply-and-demand disparities. On the other hand, predictions of the future consumer demand in terms of costs are made superfluous.

The Synchronized-Pricing Policy

The purpose in proposing to the entrepreneur a variety of techniques is to provide him with a kit of tools from which he may select those best suited to his firm, operations, and products. The techniques are presented in the order of increasing applicability and decreasing directness.

The synchronized-pricing policy and its twin technique, the open-price ordering policy, are designed to ensure that the obstacles to the free operation of the price mechanism are removed. There are a variety of ways that this can be accomplished. Experience will show which measures are most successful under what combinations of circumstances.

Probably no single technique can be relied on to secure complete results in all situations. Rather it is desirable to apply jointly several of the policies. By relaying all price fluctuations instantly and accurately to the extreme markets, the twin techniques comply with the second principle of economic efficiency.

It is essential that each procedure require the minimum amount of change from present practices. For that purpose, their deficiencies must be pinpointed. What is it, in what the entrepreneur does, that wreaks havoc with the economy? Two defects can be identified: the interception, lag, or deflection of price fluctuations in their progress through marketing channels, and the time interval, at each stage, between the purchase and sale of individual units of merchandise. To overcome these defects, two measures are proposed: a pricing policy devised to straddle the points of defective transmission of price fluctuations, and a reordering procedure designed to reduce to zero the time interval between purchase and sale. The first measure is designated the *synchronized-pricing policy;* the second, the *open-price ordering policy.*

The synchronized-pricing policy consists of taking into account when buying and selling goods current fluctuations in the consumer demand, as well as in raw-material and intermediate costs. That policy conforms to the prerequisites for the free operation of the price mechanism and particularly for the instant and accurate transmission of all price fluctuations to the extreme markets. This is a difficult assignment for everyone involved; it may be decentralized by having every firm watch only the immediately adjacent markets. If this is done at all stages of the pipeline on a weekly or biweekly basis and selling prices are revised accordingly, price changes should be reasonably well synchronized.

The synchronized-pricing policy requires frequent vertical contact with suppliers and clients. If all firms within a given pipeline agree to provide their principal clients with changing cost information, this will be sufficient. Many suppliers already mail revised price lists to their clients.

With the synchronized-pricing policy, there is no need to predict the consumer demand in terms of anticipated costs. Risk and market uncertainty are reduced to a minimum. Among the three pricing policies, this is the only one from which positive and assured results may be expected.

I suggested earlier that functions of that nature are prime candidates for automation. Frequently revised price lists may consist of updated computer runs. These will assist clients in deciding whether and when to buy, how much to bid when the price is subject to negotiation, how much to order at one time, and how frequently to reorder.

The object of the synchronized-pricing policy is economic stability—not through the rigid control of prices but through the free operation of the price mechanism. Under the present system, which comprises many rigidities (some intended to stabilize prices), prices vary in certain economies from simple to double without external causes. Through observance of the synchronized-pricing policy, prices left to themselves may be expected to vary within much narrower limits. Lost stability can only be recovered through minute price fluctuations; thus, for the sake of general stability, retail prices, raw-material prices, and all intermediate prices should be allowed to move freely.

A good illustration is the balance of the bicycle rider. That balance is the result of minute motions of the front wheel to the right and to the left, while the general direction remains approximately rectilinear. But if, for any reason, the handlebar should be hindered from moving freely, the effect would almost certainly be a loss of balance, which, because it could not be corrected, would translate into a spill. The very same principle applies to the operation of the price mechanism. It, too, requires, in order to achieve and maintain a cross-stage balance between supply and demand, that minute fluctuations be permitted to manifest themselves and be freely transmitted to all stages.

While the synchronized-pricing policy is designed to promote fluidity of prices, it is not quite the equivalent of vertical integration, production to order, or replacement pricing. It has a weakness. Producers and merchants buy in large quantities and rather infrequently, whereas their sales are generally continuous. When a sale occurs at a time when costs or the consumer demand (or both) differ from what they were at the time of the purchase, the income in relation to expenditures is altered and the profit margin distorted. It is that weakness which the open-price ordering policy is designed to overcome.

The Open-Price Ordering Policy

To reduce price fluctuations intervening between the purchase and sale of given units of merchandise, it is desirable to shorten the time lapse between them. If the time can be compressed to zero, the price fluctuations are canceled. Costs and selling prices being based on identical market conditions, there can be no distortion in profit margins.

The object is to make the day of the sale of each unit coincide with the day of its purchase (or the purchase of its elements). The physical flow of goods can remain what it is today. This is possible when the pricing of goods is divorced from their physical progress through the pipeline. The purchase price and selling price must be based on identical data, and that is possible when the two prices are determined simultaneously.

To reduce the time interval between purchases and sales, the frequency of ordering is increased. Orders are placed at a rate approximating the frequency of sales, without affecting the autonomous rhythm of the flow of merchandise. From the standpoint of pricing, orders can be more frequent (the size of each order being correspondingly reduced); from that of shipping, deliveries can combine units covered by a number of consecutive purchase orders. Thus shipping charges remain optimized.

Orders are placed at the same rhythm as sales are made. Eight units sold prompt an order for eight units. Practical considerations dictate the frequency of reordering. Once a day is the theoretical target, but once a week may be less cumbersome, and even biweekly reorders may be acceptable. If the firm has twelve units in its inventory, each unit is reordered the day (or week) it is sold. This means, according to the FIFO principle, that a thirteenth unit is ordered at the time the first unit is sold.

With an increased frequency of ordering, there remains a problem of obtaining unit prices as favorable for orders involving small quantities as those for much larger orders. The open-price ordering policy takes care of that problem.

In a nonspeculative economy where no purchasing power is wasted and no sales resistance generated, it is scarcely necessary for supplier and client to confirm agreements with formal contracts. A cancellation does not mean the loss of a sale but an opportunity to serve the next customer. The most modest orders are gratefully accepted. The aggregate propensity to consume is adequate to take up all of the potential national production.

It may be years before all of the purchasing power now going to waste is recovered. For that reason, today's entrepreneur needs to continue using precautions while applying policies tending to reduce the waste. Among these precautions is the conventional contract between supplier and client. What is needed is a redesigned instrument of trade that is sound for use in a modern industrial economy as well as in the sick economy in which business must still be transacted. The open-price ordering policy makes use of a form of contract consisting of two independent parts—one part permanent and the other finite but repetitive. The first is an empty shell; it spells out the names and addresses of supplier and client, gives complete specification of the product (model, quality, size, weight, color, and so on), stipulates that all prices will be established in accordance with the synchronized-pricing policy, indicates minimum quantities to be shipped at one time and method of shipment, and the frequency of reordering. It leaves out date, quantities, and prices. The second part of the contract consists of individual purchase orders, written in close coincidence with sales. These spell out the quantity, unit price, total price, date of ordering, and date of delivery. Together the two instruments have legal force. Furthermore they lend confidence to the supplier, who should be disposed to extend discounts on the basis of the annual (or quarterly) volume rather than of individual orders.

If the synchronized-pricing policy and open-price ordering policy are carefully observed, selling prices are based on current production and marketing costs, as well as on the current rate of accrual of the consumer demand. Cost changes are transmitted to all firms in the pipeline with a minimum of delay. If, for each batch of units sold, a replacement batch is ordered at all stages, fluctuations in consumer demand are automatically transmitted to the whole succession of suppliers.

The optimum frequency of reordering is subject to experimentation. Maximum net savings obtained in the long run through application of the technique, after deduction of the costs incurred, will be a deciding factor.

Sales volume can also be substituted for the frequency of ordering. Whenever a predetermined dollar volume has been sold, a corresponding volume is reordered. The result should be approximately identical. It may even be possible to substitute the instant and accurate transmission of volume fluctuations for price fluctuations, with similar results.

The ordering procedure is considerably simplified under the two new policies. The placing of individual orders tends to become automatic. The risk and market uncertainty being reduced to a minimum, the need for conjecturing and speculating vanishes. Business administration is made easier. The large element of personal judgment and foresight, so necessary in business today, should decrease considerably. The cost of management is reduced in proportion.

The synchronized-pricing policy and open-price ordering policy are applicable to a wide array of firms, operations, and products. Applicability is maximized, although some benefits may be somewhat less certain. If the frequency of reordering is spaced out from daily to weekly and in some instances to biweekly or monthly, obviously results cannot be exactly identical. Nevertheless, the interminable inflationary or deflationary price trends of the past will be effectively checked and reversed before they have time to do much harm.

In combination, the promotion of models 2 and 3 and of the three policies described in this chapter can be depended on to achieve high levels of efficiency. Free capitalist economies should become transformed for the better.

Transition Period

In a healthy economy, there would be no risk of unfavorable side effects from applying the recommended procedures, but our economy is not healthy. Business must still be transacted in an atmosphere of excessive competitive pressure. And although it is the object of the procedures to reduce that pressure, the first firms to apply them will continue to feel the weight of defective methods used by others. Wisdom and tact are required in the selection of techniques. Those techniques should be applied, first, that experience has proved favorable to the development of the enterprise.

Additional policies may become safe with the passage of time, until the treatment can be administered full strength. The time element is paramount in this evolution, which may extend over a period of years. The initial patience should be rewarded in subsequent stages.

10 Auxiliary Policies

This chapter examines a completely different set of policies. Called auxiliary policies (the earlier measures are specific), they have no therapeutic properties. They are aimed at reinforcing the benefits of the specific techniques once the price mechanism has been liberated.

The auxiliary policies have long been advocated; in a speculative multistage economy, they remain impractical and ineffectual. When some potential purchasing power has been recovered, their application should become feasible and profitable. They concern price (fluidity, proportionality), production (acceleration, flexibility), and protective measures (monopolies, tariffs).

Price and Wage Fluidity

Prices and wage rates are inclined to be rigid in a speculative economy. Profit-margin distortions prevent the cross-stage synchronization of supply and demand flows; static supply-and-demand disparities and the accompanying waste of purchasing power generate excessive competitive pressure.

Price rigidities result from the plight of sellers to maintain price levels no lower than those once obtained, and buyers to continue to receive goods at prices no higher than those once paid. Wage rigidities are the effect of the tug-of-war between workers clinging to wage rates once received and management holding on to wage levels once accepted by labor. Under the circumstances, price and wage fluidity is precluded. Much as some or all parties might desire it, they cannot afford it.

For the same reasons of insufficient consumer purchasing power and excessive competition, employers have exploited marginal workers by offering them low wages. Government has intervened by instituting minimum hourly wage rates, a solution that has actually increased the ranks of the unemployed.

In addition to competition-related rigidities, there are purely mechanical limitations to the free play of prices and wages. One manufacturing firm indicates that every price revision for its line of merchandise costs $120,000, so it tries to hold the frequency of revisions to once or twice a year.

The practice of price setting, whether at retail or wholesale, militates against prices gravitating toward levels at which cross-stage supply-and-demand equation can be attained. As a result, the allocation of scarce resources is a mockery in a modern industrial economy. Manufacturer-fixed or manufacturer-suggested retail prices are another form of price rigidity.

Utility rates, transportation rates, and insurance premiums are subject to the control of utility and other federal or state regulating commissions. This slows down price adjustments. In addition, mechanical limitations to price changes abound. Telephone pay stations, coin-operated vending machines, rapid-transit systems, and similar services make price changes awkward and slow. Other limitations to price and wage fluidity are common.

The worst form of rigidity is that willfully maintained so as to retain the confidence of the clientele. That is a purely artificial brand of price stability, with no assurance of permanence. It leads to overreaction if tensions become unbearable. The clientele would gain more lasting confidence if prices were fluid and therefore remained on their own accord within narrow boundaries. And if as a result of price fluidity, competitive pressures subsided to where competition were neutral, there would be no need to pamper clients since consumer demand would tend to be insatiable.

Price and wage fluidity cannot be attained in the current atmosphere. It is not until some of the specific policies have been adopted and tensions relieved that a policy of fluidity in arriving at fair (though freely changing) price and wage levels has a chance of being applied. When that occurs, fluidity will have a double effect: it will help entrepreneurs maximize profits beyond levels attainable today and will promote the objectives of the specific policies. Price and wage fluidity is a requisite for free operation of the price mechanism.

Proportionality of Cost to Sales Volume

In a modern industrial economy, the aggregate profit margin in the consumer's dollar is not allocated in balanced proportions to successive stages. Profit margins tend to rise and fall periodically and progressively at successive stages of the economic pipeline. The higher profit margins crowd alternately toward retail markets or toward raw-material markets. As a result, the flow of supply never quite matches the rate of the consumer demand on retail markets. Inventories accumulate or dry up at intervals.

As long as that state of affairs endures, profit margins do not perform efficiently their assigned function of allocating scarce resources among avid customers. All firms operate in a business atmosphere of excessive competitive pressure; they scarcely have an inducement to switch from one excessive product to another, the demand for which is almost equally stagnant. When sales resistance is encountered regardless of the line of merchandise, the product mix remains essentially unchanged.

When, however, a substantial portion of the potential consumer purchasing power has been recovered, a different complexion comes over business.

To an oversupply of some goods invariably corresponds an undersupply of some others. Under the circumstances, it pays to heed the signals of fluctuating profit margins. These have meaning and permit the maximization of profits over and above levels attainable today. The product mix is altered to match the consumer demand more accurately.

As long as a general tendency toward saturated markets prevails, there is no particular reason why costs should be proportional to the volume of business. All costs are too high and all income from sales too low; profit margins are constantly threatened. But as soon as an insatiable consumer demand manifests itself, a more accurate match between supply and demand can be attained if costs are proportional to the volume of business. What is meant is that the proportion of variable costs should increase in relation to fixed costs.

In certain industries, that appears at first either impossible or uneconomical. But a number of measures can be used to make costs more nearly proportional to supply volume. Fixed costs can be allocated to units handled. The problem is not so much one of a deficiency of production facilities (which can usually be expanded if the demand justifies the investment), as one of an oversupply of productive resources, which may remain idle during prolonged periods of time. To avoid productive capacity remaining idle when the purchasing power is adequate, all that is necessary is to have in readiness an alternate line of products that can be manufactured in existing facilities. There will be no more general glut, only individual goods in oversupply while others are deficient. Versatility, or planning for alternate product lines, permits costs to be more nearly proportional to volumes produced. The same is true in distribution channels.

Acceleration of Production and Distribution

Sometimes hesitation, indecision, and procrastination accompany production and distribution operations subjected to the threats of market uncertainty, sales resistance, and excessive competitive pressure. When that threat is removed, there is no reason to be overcautious. The entrepreneur proceeds with confidence; he cannot go far wrong as long as he watches his profit margins. Someone, somewhere, will want his product. If his profit margin tends to erode for a given product, that for another will encourage him to make a switch.

There is no particular virtue in speed as such except as it cuts costs when all indications are favorable. The duration of the so-called production-and-distribution cycle (not to be confused with the business cycle), which varies greatly among commodities, is not among the causes of business cycles. If price fluctuations were freely relayed to all stages and supply flows adjusted to parallel the demand on all markets, the length of time required in getting goods from mines and fields to retail shelves would be irrelevant. It remains true that an optimum utilization of material, financial, and human resources admits of no unnecessary waste of time. It is in that sense that expediting production and distribution operations will represent a substantial advantage.

Increased Flexibility of Production and Distribution

This is another policy that has little appeal today but will take on increased significance as specific policies are applied. It will then become possible to meet the changing consumer demand with much greater accuracy than is now feasible. The entrepreneur will maximize his profits beyond levels attainable at present. But increased profits will require considerable flexibility in production and distribution rates.

The present lack of flexibility in production and distribution rates is a symptom of rigidity. A decision is made on the basis of expectations to produce or purchase merchandise. Since sales resistance attaches to the great majority of consumer goods, the switch from one overabundant product to another is scarcely warranted. By pushing sales hard enough, the entrepreneur can sell almost anything.

The outlook may be quite different when specific policies have succeeded in liberating the operation of the price mechanism. For every overabundant product, there exist one or more products in short supply. It will then be worthwhile to switch from the production or procurement of goods in excess supply to that of goods in deficient supply. The switch is desirable if profits are to be maximized.

A fluctuation in profit margins will signal that a given supply is now insufficient or excessive and that in order for the supply to be synchronized with the demand, a switch is indicated. The fluctuation will invite a correction. An adjustment in the rate of production or distribution may tend to reestablish cross-stage equilibrium. Since the fluctuation affects almost simultaneously all stages in the pipeline, the entire flow, from raw materials to finished goods, is synchronized with itself, as well as with the accruing consumer demand— that is, if production and distribution rates are flexible.

Entrepreneurs will develop a sensitiveness to fluctuations in profit margins for their products. They will want to make the necessary changes by reallocating their facilities and resources in response to their profit margins. This will promote the accurate regulation of production and distribution to match the changing volume of the consumer demand.

Industrial production can be made more flexible through the acceleration or deceleration of the speed of production, by varying the number of shifts, the number of workers per shift, and the number of weekly work hours per worker. The optimum utilization of production capacity is maintained by substituting alternate products for those in excess supply. As long as overproduction tends to be general, a policy of substitution is scarcely applicable. It will become feasible and desirable when the aggregate purchasing power approaches the nation's capacity to produce.

Industrial operations can be organized into production units. A portion of these, which may not be utilized continuously for the main product, are set up so as to be convertible to the production of alternate (though technologically related) merchandise. As soon as the demand for the regular product falls, the amortization of capital invested in buildings and equipment, as well as the overhead, is charged to alternate products. Manpower can continue to be employed, the turnover being kept to a minimum. A small contingent of workers, those assigned to the marginal units, can be trained to perform substitute operations under the guidance of competent supervisory personnel. Thus, the continuity of employment is protected.

Flexibility is not so easily introduced into agricultural pursuits. In single-crop areas, cultures should be diversified. It is not wise to let a change in demand, whatever its cause, affect the main source of revenue of entire populations. A marginal proportion of the farmland should be allocated to alternate cultures. Optimum operation mixes are those determined on the basis of fluctuating profit margins. Reserves of grain can be established to compensate for the irregularity of crops and cushion the inelasticity of seasonal production. These measures are not novel, but in a synchronized and stabilized economy, they are likely to be more successful and more effective.

Distribution operations traditionally are set up for a high degree of versatility and flexibility. The amortization of floor space and the overhead can be charged to high-profit merchandise. Personnel trained to handle a diversity of products can remain at work without interruption.

When wasted purchasing power is recovered and sales no longer must be pushed, distribution functions may be simplified. This will release resources, which can be utilized to increase production. Flexibility will require the conversion of commercial to industrial facilities and the retraining of sales personnel for production jobs.

Abandonment of Monopolistic Practices

The entrepreneur who finds it difficult to maintain a sufficient profit margin to survive often seeks the protection of some form of monopoly. Monopoly need not be illegal or even unethical. Copyrights, trademarks, patents, and sales promotion through product differentiation are legitimate devices to protect a business undertaking. However, every form of monopoly, legal or illegal, restrains trade and thereby wastes consumer purchasing power.

How can the race toward protection be reversed? Antitrust legislation can certainly thwart some abuses but will never eradicate the desire for protection or subtle attempts at circumventing the law. A more fundamental approach will be needed to reduce permanently the propensity to seek monopolistic protection. Suppose that some of the policies advocated in chapter 9 have been applied for a sufficient period of time and a substantial portion of potential purchasing power has been reclaimed; this might eventually reinstate the full force of Say's Law, according to which supply creates its own demand.

When that happens, the reasons for seeking monopolistic protection will tend to vanish. The protection will cease to appear attractive. In time it will be abandoned. In an economy in which every unit produced finds a customer without need for a sales effort, competitive pressure becomes neutral: the demand equals the supply. Under the circumstances, there will be no advantage to product differentiation, threatening types of advertising, or high-pressure salesmanship. Such practices will be dropped by the wayside. Entrepreneurs will be able, in the long run, to make more money without them. When that time comes, business managers should not hesitate to throw away the crutches of monopolistic practices.

Abandonment of Tariff Protection

Four hundred years ago, the mercantilists advocated international free trade. Even today, when free trade is difficult to achieve, many believe that free trade would be desirable and are working on reducing tariffs. The problem is closely associated with that of excessive competitive pressure on domestic markets. When national markets are saturated, foreign markets often can provide outlets for surplus goods. At times, however, foreign markets themselves are oversupplied, and the confluence of commodities of foreign origin irks domestic producers who are undersold. This makes for international tensions, one nation rising tariffs on certain goods in retaliation for another nation's tariffs on others. Excessive competitive pressure is thus exported to rival economies, with the result that economic conflicts become political conflicts. Under the circumstances, it is difficult to make progress in the direction of international free trade.

But when rational marketing policies have been applied for a reasonable period in two or more nations and competitive pressure has been neutralized in each, foreign markets will no longer be sought as dumping grounds for surplus merchandise. On the contrary, foreign goods will be solicited to supplement domestic assortments, and each participating nation will benefit from mutual exchanges. This permits the most productive kind of exchanges across national boundaries and promotes healthy political relations.

A policy of international free trade is a desirable goal that cannot be achieved in today's economic climate. As long as most industrial nations are burdened with excessive competitive pressure and purchasing power is insufficient to take up all that can be produced, tariff protection appears inevitable. The day may come, however, when the excessive pressure recedes; it will then be beneficial to cancel all tariffs.

11 Hints for Public Policy

The entrepreneur is responsible for modern economic ills. The science of economics had not advanced far enough to bring to his attention the microeconomic sources of inefficiency, stagnation, and instability. It is within his power to adapt his policies and practices to the needs of the day instead of continuing to operate as though we were still living in the Golden Age. The Industrial Revolution has changed the structure and modalities of production and distribution, and the entrepreneur must now learn to adapt his ways to changed conditions.

Role of the Government

The sooner the government puts its house in order, the more favorable will be the business climate in which the entrepreneurial adaptations are to be accomplished. Politicians should balance the budget and initiate a program to repay the national debt. The government must also observe a hands-off policy to avoid interfering in any way with the adaptation process.

When a better business atmosphere has been established and entrepreneurs have succeeded in carrying out a sufficient portion of their adaptation program, the need for protection through legislation will begin to subside. It will then be safe and wise for Congress to repeal those acts that have limited competition, thereby inviting unemployment and stagflation.

When currently wasted purchasing power has been recovered so that the effective consumer demand approaches the nation's capacity to produce, the restrictions imposed by various laws of the past can be revoked without danger. Healthy competition for sales as well as for jobs may then lead to much improved allocation of resources. Say's Law may again be valid, and selfish actions of entrepreneurs may then truly contribute to the well-being of society.

If, however, the government wishes to participate more actively in the adaptation process, it can disseminate the new knowledge to those concerned: the profession of producers (farmers, miners, fishermen, manufacturers, assemblers), distributors (wholesalers, jobbers, commodity brokers, retailers), and financiers. Larger firms will want to know every detail of the new theory: they have staffs that can understand it. They will also be among the first to reap the fruits of the recommended policies. The smaller firms may not need to understand the abstract theory but are capable of imitating the leaders. They only need to be told what to do and how to do it.

The government can be helpful in the educational effort necessary to disseminate the information to the masses. Conferences, courses, seminars, and radio and television programs can be sponsored by the Treasury, Commerce, Interior, and Agriculture departments. Publications, pamphlets, and cassettes can be issued.

Research

Finally, although it may not be necessary to do additional research before launching a program of applications of sounder policies and practices, it will be of interest to continue the investigations in several directions. The government may wish to include in its program of basic and applied research the simulation of the flows of supply and demand through the economic pipeline, in accordance with the ideas suggested in chapter 6. This may be done with fictitious figures and then with historical data. Procedures and policies proposed in chapters 8 and 9 could be evaluated. It may be of interest to a private firm to find out whether it would be better off today if it had applied such procedures and policies two or three years earlier. If the computer gives an affirmative answer, the firm will be encouraged to proceed with the application of some of the recommended measures.

Additional research of interest might be empirical studies pertaining to vertical integration versus vertical specialization, the proportion of products produced and distributed speculatively versus nonspeculatively, and methods of buying, selling, pricing, and ordering. Comparisons of profit margins at successive stages in alternating phases of the cycle may illustrate the effect of lags and inaccuracies in the relay of price fluctuations. Fluctuations in inventory levels may be indicative of a lack of synchronization between supply-and-demand velocities throughout the pipeline. These and similar subjects could be included in a basic research program.

As for applied research, it may be useful to conduct a number of computer tests to determine the best mix of policies for given firms, stages, operations, and products. The recommended techniques may gain from being modified for application under varying circumstances. The optimum solution can be established by trial and error at the paper stage rather than in actuality. In all these tests, controls should be used for comparison of results. Pilot applications can be scheduled, followed by more comprehensive implementations. Such a basic and applied research program could be sponsored by the government.

12 Case Studies

Are the theory and policies presented in this book germane and relevant to the conduct of business in real life? In answer to this question, a survey was undertaken to provide an interface between abstract analysis and synthesis, on one hand, and reality, on the other; to determine whether any of the policies are already being utilized in industry and business; and to judge whether the policies are practical and economical. Two types of firms were included in the case studies: a medium-sized industrial firm exemplifying production and a large department store representing distribution.

Production

A representative manufacturing enterprise of medium size was chosen as an example of the production function. In order to make sure that no relevant data would be omitted from the investigation, a questionnaire was prepared and administered orally to volunteering executives.

Questionnaire for the Diagnostic Survey of a Manufacturing Enterprise

A. General Character of the Establishment

1. What is the company's present capitalization?

2. What is the annual sales volume?

3. How many establishments of the same type are there in the United States with an equal or higher sales volume?

4. What is the average income level of the company's patrons?

5. What is, dollarwise, the proportion of: (a) commodities used in manufacturing and procured from firms over which the company has some sort of control and (b) manufactured products that the company sells direct to ultimate consumers?

6. What proportion of the company's business goes to mail-order houses?

7. Is the company affected by economic stagnation or instability?

8. Does the company have a problem in predicting the future demand for its products?

9. Is the company interested in solving these two problems?

10. Does the company have any suggestions as to how these two problems can effectively be solved?

B. Degree of Vertical Specialization

11. What are the main classes of products manufactured?

12. Indicate, for leading products, the total number of successive stages at which separate firms handle the products, their parts, or the materials required for their manufacture. Include in the count the stage of the mines and fields at one end, and the stage of the retailers at the other. The total number of stages will then correspond to that of consecutive markets and transactions.

13. Indicate whether any individual firm is so compartmentalized that one division buys from another. For all intents and purposes, such divisions represent independent enterprises and should be counted as separate stages.

14. Indicate instances in which, for any products, the total number of successive stages (enterprises or divisions) varies as between suppliers or between clients.

15. Does the company have a policy or a plan to increase the degree of vertical integration?

16. What are the possibilities of mergers with suppliers or clients, or of acquiring or controlling the assets of suppliers or clients?

C. Proportion of Speculative Production and/or Distribution

17. What is, dollarwise, the proportion of goods put into production by the company only after receipt of clients' orders?

18. What proportion of materials and parts is produced by the company's suppliers only after receipt of the company's orders? What part of that proportion is produced in company-owned or -controlled plants?

19. What proportion of materials or parts is produced by the company's suppliers only after receipt of orders from the company's clients? What part of that proportion is produced in company-owned or -controlled plants?

20. Does the ultimate consumer have an opportunity to place an advance order (prior to manufacture) at a saving?

21. What is, dollarwise, the proportion of goods whose selling prices are periodically revised to be in line with replacement costs?

22. How frequently are replacement costs (a) requested, (b) received?

23. How soon after a change in replacement costs is the company's purchasing officer informed of the change?

24. How soon after a change in replacement costs are selling prices adjusted to reflect the change?

25. Do suppliers give any assurance that price lists will be honored until replaced, or are prices subject to change without notice?

26. Dollarwise, what proportion of materials or parts is ordered with the understanding that price lists will be honored? What proportion of finished goods is offered for sale by suppliers with price lists guaranteed until replaced?

27. Once a selling price change has been decided upon by the company, how long does it take for a new price list to be prepared, printed, and mailed?

28. What is the fastest that a price change can be communicated by the company to its clients?

D. Pricing Policy

29. In determining buying and selling prices and in deciding whether, what, when, how much, and in what price range to buy, does the company follow a consistent pricing policy? Merchandise subject to price fixing is not to be taken into account here.

30. What is, dollarwise, the proportion of transactions conducted by the company in compliance with the short-term (shortsighted) pricing policy, taking into account current price changes on the two adjacent markets only?

31. What is, dollarwise, the proportion of transactions conducted by the company in compliance with the speculative-pricing policy, taking into account anticipated price changes (a) on the retail market, the raw-material market, and all intermediate markets; (b) on the two adjacent markets?

32. What is, dollarwise, the proportion of transactions conducted by the company in compliance with the synchronized-pricing policy, taking into account current price changes (a) on the raw-material market, the retail market, and all intermediate markets; (b) on the two adjacent markets?

33. What is, dollarwise, the proportion of transactions conducted by the company in compliance with a conscious, deliberate, and consistent combination of the previously mentioned three pricing policies?

34. What is, dollarwise, the proportion of transactions conducted by the company on an opportunistic basis, without regard to any pricing policy?

35. What is, dollarwise, the proportion of transactions conducted by the company on any other basis—and on what basis or bases?

36. How does the company secure information on current price changes on the raw-material market, the retail market, and all intermediate markets?

37. Does the company utilize such information as may be available—and how is it used?

38. Does the company make a systematic effort to secure information on price changes at all stages?

39. If such information were available to the company, would it be utilized—and how would it be used?

E. Ordering Practices

40. What is the average life of a purchase order? of a selling contract?

41. What is the average annual number of purchases? of sales?

42. For a given time period, what is the average ratio of the number of purchases to the number of sales?

43. Do purchase or sales contracts ever call for staggered deliveries? If so, assuming that delivery dates and quantities are specified, are provisions ever made for prices on future deliveries to be revised at the time of each delivery?

44. Do such contracts ever carry escalator clauses or price redetermination clauses?

45. Do suppliers insist on (a) large individual orders or (b) guarantees of minmum annual volume before extending prices and discounts corresponding to the annual volume of business? Does the company do the same?

46. Is it possible for the company to reorder a little at a time, in replacement of units sold, and still get favorable prices and discounts? Does the company make this possible for its clients?

47. How frequently could the company reorder without taxing the ordering facilities or making the cost of handling such reorders prohibitive?

48. Indicate, for the more important classes of products, typical delivery times, from the date of mailing the order to the receipt of merchandise.

49. May the company cancel its orders? Does the company accept cancellations from its clients?

F. Other Marketing Practices

50. What is, dollarwise, the approximate proportion of merchandise subject to manufacturer-suggested retail prices?

51. What is, dollarwise, the approximate proportion of merchandise otherwise subject to price fixing?

52. What is, dollarwise, the approximate proportion of merchandise purchased—and of merchandise sold—at flexible, fluid, often adjusted prices, versus rigid, pegged, stable prices?

53. Are the company's incoming and outgoing inventory levels essentially proportioned to requirements determined by delivery periods and average sales volumes?

54. Is the physical flow of merchandise from the raw-material producers to the consumer steady and even, or spasmodic and halting?

55. How does the company measure the supply-and-demand relationship?

Summary of Responses

Responses are so worded that the reader does not have to refer to the questionnaire. P = Purchasing Division, M = Marketing Division.

A. General Character of the Establishment

1. Net assets are $80 million.

2. Annual sales are $150 million.

3. The largest competitor has annual sales of $85 million.

4. The income level of patrons ranges from $25,000 to $55,000.

5. P: The proportion of commodities procured from firms controlled by the company is 0 percent. M: The proportion of products sold direct to consumers is 0 percent.

6. The proportion of business sold to mail-order houses is $2 million, or 1 1/3 percent.

7. The company, producing a line of luxury items, is affected by economic instability.

8. Forecasting is difficult; the prediction of the optimal product mix, involving styles and colors, is a problem.

9. The company is interested in solving both problems.

10. The company does not have a good solution. There are no industry-wide statistics; the firm has to do its own market research. In a recession, earnings are hurt more than sales. The cost of excessive inventories prompts the company to promote sales actively.

B. Degree of Vertical Specialization

11. Products are divided into three main classes: A (68 percent), B (20 percent), and C (10 percent).

12. The number of stages is very low. The company is highly integrated. P: Three stages are involved; with few exceptions, the company buys from primary producers. M: It sells direct to retailers (never to consumers).

13. P: One supplier is compartmentalized in that he operates an autonomous plant to transform commodities used by the company. M: No compartmentalization exists at the retail level. Within the company, three separate facilities contribute parts later fed to the assembly plant.

14. The company does not know the total number of stages because its operations are not affected.

15. The company is highly integrated. P: There is a possibility for further automation, which would be cheaper and would assure the needed supply. Also, the takeover of one operation is possible and has been discussed.

16. The possibilities of mergers with suppliers or clients are nil. Acquisitions of assets of suppliers may be slightly more feasible.

C. Proportion of Speculative Production and/or Distribution

17. The proportion of production to order is negligible, about 1 percent for special orders.

18. The proportion of commodities produced to order by suppliers is not known.

19. No commodities are produced by suppliers to the order of the company's clients.

20. Consumers do not have an opportunity to place advance orders at a saving.

21. The proportion of goods whose selling prices are revised in line with replacement costs is 0 percent. There is no periodical price revision. All prices are maintained for one year.

22. Replacement costs are not requested.

23. The purchasing officer is not informed of changes in replacement costs. He takes the initiative in ascertaining cost changes.

24. Selling prices are adjusted every twelve months, regardless of changes in replacement costs.

25. Suppliers' price lists are guaranteed, except for a few commodities which are priced at shipping time. Vendors may give a thirty to sixty day warning of upcoming cost changes.

26. P: The proportion of commodities ordered with the understanding that price lists will be honored is 95 percent. M: All of finished goods are offered with price lists guaranteed until replaced (for twelve months).

27. Selling prices are changed once a year, and there is no problem about sending out revised price lists.

28. There is no problem in advising clients of price changes; this is done every twelve months.

D. Pricing Policy

29. P: Buying prices are indirectly influenced by decisions reached by the Marketing Division. For certain commodities, quantities purchased are decided on the basis of volume discounts. Otherwise there is no particular pricing policy in effect in the Purchasing Division. M: Besides the annual revision of selling prices, the company's pricing policy differs according to the clientele. Department stores and specialty stores use a suggested 50 percent markup, subject to periodic promotions. Catalogue showrooms and discount houses receive a differentiated product line, with a 30 to 35 percent markup and less promotion. Mail-order chains receive branded merchandise carrying a private label, as well as special merchandise with no promotion, at 8 percent below the regular wholesale price.

30. The short-term pricing policy is not used by the company. P: For one thing, there is no relation between raw-material costs and finished-good selling prices. M: The staff estimates costs for the next twelve months, looks at competition, and sets prices. Fixed costs are impossible to allo-

cate. The company never reduces set prices, but it will promote. A fixed quantity of goods is set aside for annual or semiannual promotions. About 45 percent of the merchandise is sold below the wholesale list price.

31. The speculative pricing policy is used practically 100 percent of the time. The company makes forecasts of material costs so that it can make financial plans. Advance buying to avoid a price increase is limited to one or two months' supply.

32. The synchronized pricing policy is not used. The company buys on the raw-material market; thus, there is no problem of synchronization at the purchasing end.

33. The company's pricing policy is consistent. Because of the highly controlled environment, the speculative pricing policy is used almost exclusively.

34. Except for special pricing terms granted two or three times a year, it can be said that opportunistic pricing is never used.

35. No other pricing policy is used.

36. The company secures information on current price changes on the raw-material and retail markets, from trade publications, as well as from the competition.

37. Available data are used for forecasting raw-material costs. Because of OPEC's price boosts, all selling prices had to be revised several times at midyear.

38. P: The company secures data on raw-material price changes from the suppliers themselves. These will reveal price trends but not their profits. M: Retail prices of the competition are followed.

39. Data would be used as indicated previously.

E. Ordering Practices

40. The average life of a contract varies: P: Purchase orders, never for multiple deliveries, are closed on delivery. Some major commodities are contracted for on a yearly basis for volume discounts; prices and amounts remain flexible. M: Selling contracts run for one year at a fixed price subject to change with thirty-day notice. Delivery dates vary, but the supply is guaranteed.

41. The annual number of purchases and sales is unknown. P: Separate purchase orders are written for 1,500 materials or parts, making for thousands of orders. M: The number of annual sales is not available.

42. The ratio of purchases to sales is unknown. P: Purchase orders vary greatly. M: Retailers order monthly or semiannually, the average being sixty days.

43. P: Staggered deliveries are not called for in purchase orders. M: In selling, contracts are used only for private-label merchandise, for three months, stating price and total quantity. Individual orders are placed against such contracts, specifying quantities and delivery dates. Prices are not revised on delivery.

44. No escalation clauses are inserted in contracts.

45. P: Minimum purchase orders and discounts vary. In each case, a study is made to optimize saving versus investment. Maximum discounts correspond to supplies for one to six months. M: In selling, the company allows no volume discounts, though it offers free freight for truckload quantities.

46. P: A few suppliers will give discounts on the basis of annual purchases. The company would prefer this but often cannot obtain it. Besides, a front-end discount is better than a refund at the end of twelve months. M: In selling, the company has a policy of shipping no fewer than ten pieces. This makes it possible for the client to reorder in replacement of units sold.

47. The frequency of reordering is limited more by losing volume discounts than by the cost of paperwork.

48. Typical delivery times average one week, both in purchasing and in shipping finished goods. P: For manufactured parts made to specifications, a lead time of eight to twelve weeks must be added to the delivery time. No lead time is added for raw materials.

49. P: The company does not have the right to cancel a purchase order. Material responsibility means that the company must reimburse expenses incurred by the supplier. M: On the other hand, the client can cancel an order until shipped. Unsold goods may also be returned if bought for a special sales event.

F. Other Marketing Practices

50. Manufacturer-suggested prices are used.

51. Suggested prices are used for most products, except those sold to catalogue showrooms and discount houses.

52. Are prices flexible or rigid? P: Raw-material price lists are good for three to six months, until renegotiated. Raw materials increase by less than the inflation rate. M: Price lists for finished goods are valid for six to twelve months. Selling prices are never reduced, although promotions are held.

53. P: Incoming inventory levels are predetermined on the basis of marketing plans. For the sake of production efficiency, production rates are smoothed according to marketing experience. Inventories are revised to make this possible. Also, a cost analysis indicates optimum levels in terms of discounts and investments. M: Outgoing inventories are kept at a thirty-day supply level, computed on a twelve-month moving average. The company never speculates. There is always a danger of obsolescence.

54. P: The flow of merchandise from raw materials to consumer is steady, except for curtailment due to the recession. M: The volume, not price, varies each month. Promotions help to sell. Monthly forecasts determine production; production schedules dictate purchase orders.

55. Measurement of supply and demand is a trick question. It was answered as follows: The annual forecast is revised monthly and adjusted; then, the output is changed.

Recommendations

The survey has a single purpose: to liberate the operation of the price mechanism so it can effectively balance profit margins at successive stages. This implies the elimination of all impediments to the instant and accurate transmission of price fluctuations to all vertical markets. There are essentially four avenues open for that purpose: vertical integration, production and distribution to order, the synchronized-pricing policy, and the open-price ordering policy. The problem is to find practical ways to promote these.

Vertical Integration: The diagnostic survey indicates that the company is highly integrated already. Because vertical integration is very effective in achieving the purposes at hand, three additional steps are advocated:

> Recommendation 1: If otherwise feasible and economically justified, the company may wish to investigate the possibility of producing, itself, one processed material now being procured from another firm.

> Recommendation 2: Subject to the same requisites, the company may wish to investigate the possibility of manufacturing, itself, parts now being purchased from other firms. Omit items purchased in insignificant quantities and those made to order.

> Recommendation 3: When it is felt that an optimum degree of vertical integration has been reached, it may be helpful to address compartmentalization within the company. For example, the company's separate manufacturing operation, unless fully integrated from the standpoint of the

accounting procedure, might receive the benefit of techniques pertaining to pricing and ordering.

Production and Distribution to Order: The survey shows that the great majority of items are produced speculatively for stock. The theory indicates that from the standpoint of liberating the relay of price fluctuations, production and distribution to order is sounder. Two measures may be considered:

Recommendation 4: Offer a modest discount to retailers willing to place advance orders, giving the company time to order materials and parts and to manufacture the desired units for future delivery. Such orders are not subject to cancellation. The share of orders obtained on that basis avoid business risk and market uncertainty, the need for predicting the future consumer demand, future costs, and the product mix. More importantly, they avoid impeding the free play of the price mechanism.

Recommendation 5: In pricing merchandise thus offered for future delivery and computing the appropriate discount rate, current demand and current costs should be taken into account.

The Synchronized-Pricing Policy: The diagnostic survey has shown that the company's selling prices are set for a twelve-month span, with occasionally a midyear revision. This does not necessarily mean that demand fluctuations are not relayed upstream. Volume changes are transmitted, and the company is aware at all times of the sales profile. Nevertheless, the allocation of profit margins can only be balanced between vertical stages by price movements. For the sake of balance in the allocation, the following modifications in present practices are submitted for consideration:

Recommendation 6: The pricing of goods destined for mail-order houses that issue new catalogues twice a year should be revised at six-month intervals.

Recommendation 7: The pricing of goods destined for catalogue showrooms and discount houses should be revised as often as these issue a new catalogue. It may be necessary to offer them a differentiated line of goods.

Recommendation 8: The frequency of revising selling prices on goods destined for department stores and specialty shops should be accelerated in several steps: first, at twelve-month, then at six-month, three-month, and finally one-month intervals. The purpose of varying frequencies is to provide experimentation and comparisons. The line of goods may have to be differentiated. It is anticipated that monthly revisions may eventually prove advantageous.

Recommendation 9: Once a schedule of frequencies of price revisions has been established, it is recommended that prices be set by the synchronized pricing policy, taking into account current demand changes and current cost changes. Another way of saying this is that prices be set on the basis of current replacement prices, both at the purchasing and the selling end. In particular, it is important that current selling prices be based not on the costs incurred in making the goods but on the costs of replacing the materials and parts needed in their production. The object is to promote the simultaneity of price fluctuations at all stages, knowing that a greater and more enduring price stability will result from it than from artificially pegged prices.

Recommendation 10: More flexibility should be designed into the price-marking procedure than exists presently. Price changes should be welcomed, not avoided, because they make for long-run price stability. Flexibility can be promoted by simplifying or even eliminating the price-marking procedure. One notable benefit of more frequent price revisions should be greater regularity in production runs and greater employment stability. Another should be, eventually, smaller losses due to recessions, for it is the purpose of the recommended measures to prevent their occurrence in the future.

Recommendation 11: The company's policy of never reducing a price once set may have merit during a period of inflation but should not stand in the way of occasionally passing on to the retailer (and consumer) possible cost reductions, as a bid for increased volume.

The Open-Price Ordering Policy: The survey has brought to light that minimum orders for maximum discounts often dictate higher-than-optimal inventory levels. A flexible form of contract, permitting a faster materials and parts stock turnover, may be advantageous in those cases.

Recommendation 12: The company may wish to suggest to suppliers the use of an open-price type contract. This instrument consists of two parts, neither of which alone is legally binding but which together permit flexibility in quantities and prices while providing legal and volume-discount protection. One part is permanent, but an empty shell simply listing the specifications of the product, minimum quantities to be shipped, method of shipment, terms of payment, and similar information, but no delivery dates, no quantities, and no prices. The other part consists of a succession of one-time purchase orders specifying only the quantity, delivery date, and price. The discount is established on the basis of annual or quarterly volume.

Distribution

A representative retail establishment was selected to supplement the manufacturing enterprise. It was a department store. Observations were limited to
selected departments so that they might be made in greater depth. A modified
questionnaire was used for application to retail establishments. These are
located at the end of the pipeline, interfacing directly with the ultimate consumer. Also, retailers do not transform the merchandise and do not carry two
separate inventories.

Questionnaire for the Diagnostic Survey of a
Retail Establishment

A. General Character of the Establishment

1. What is the company's present capitalization?

2. What is the annual sales volume?

3. How many establishments of similar type are there in the same area with
   an equal or higher sales volume?

4. What is the average income level of the company's patrons?

5. What is, dollarwise, the proportion of merchandise procured from: (a)
   wholesalers or jobbers? (b) Company-owned or -controlled factories?
   (c) Independent factories?

6. Is the company affected by economic stagnation or instability?

7. Does the company have a problem in predicting the future consumer
   demand?

8. Is the company interested in solving these two problems?

9. Does the company have any suggestions as to how these two problems
   can effectively be solved?

10. What are the main groups of departments?

B. Degree of Vertical Specialization
(All subsequent questions concern individual departments)

11. What are the principal lines of merchandise carried in the department?

12. Indicate, for leading products, the total number of successive stages at
    which separate firms handle the products, their parts, or the materials

required for their manufacture. Include in the count the stage of the mines and fields at one end and the stage of the retailers at the other. The total number of stages will then correspond to that of consecutive markets and transactions.

13. Indicate whether any individual firm is so compartmentalized that one division buys from another. For all intents and purposes, such divisions represent independent enterprises and should be counted as separate stages.

14. Indicate instances in which, for any products, the total number of successive stages (enterprises or divisions) varies as between suppliers.

15. Does the company have a policy or a plan to increase the degree of vertical integration?

16. What are the possibilities of mergers with suppliers or of acquiring or controlling the assets of suppliers?

C. Proportion of Speculative Production and/or Distribution

17. What is, dollarwise, the proportion of the merchandise ordered by the buyer only after receipt of customers' orders?

18. What is, dollarwise, the proportion of the merchandise put into production only after receipt of the company's orders? What part of that proportion is manufactured in company-owned or -controlled factories?

19. What is, dollarwise, the proportion of the merchandise put into production only after receipt by the company of its customers' orders? What part of that proportion is manufactured in company-owned or -controlled factories?

20. Does the consumer have an opportunity to place an advance order (prior to manufacture) at a saving?

21. What is, dollarwise, the proportion of merchandise whose selling prices are periodically revised to be in line with replacement costs?

22. How frequently are replacement costs (a) requested? (b) received?

23. How soon after a change in replacement costs is the buyer informed of the change?

24. How soon after a change in replacement costs are selling prices adjusted to reflect the change?

25. Do suppliers give any assurance that price lists will be honored until replaced, or are prices subject to change without notice?

26. What is, dollarwise, the proportion of merchandise purchased with the understanding that price lists will be honored?

27. Once a supplier has decided on a price change, how long does it take him to have a new price list prepared, printed, mailed and delivered to the company buyer?

28. What is the fastest that a price change can be communicated by the supplier to the company buyer?

D. Pricing Policy

29. In determining buying and selling prices and in deciding whether, what, when, how much, and in what price range to buy, does the company follow a consistent pricing policy? Merchandise subject to price fixing is not to be taken into account here.

30. What is, dollarwise, the proportion of merchandise bought in compliance with the short-term (shortsighted) pricing policy, taking into account current price changes on the adjacent markets only?

31. What is, dollarwise, the proportion of merchandise bought in compliance with the speculative-pricing policy, taking into account anticipated price changes (a) on the retail market, the raw-material market, and all intermediate markets; (b) on the two adjacent markets?

32. What is, dollarwise, the proportion of merchandise bought in compliance with the synchronized-pricing policy, taking into account current price changes (a) on the raw-material market, the retail market, and all intermediate markets; (b) on the two adjacent markets?

33. What is, dollarwise, the proportion of merchandise bought in compliance with a conscious, deliberate, and consistent combination of the previously mentioned three pricing policies?

34. What is, dollarwise, the proportion of merchandise bought on an opportunistic basis, without regard to any pricing policy?

35. What is, dollarwise, the proportion of merchandise bought on any other basis, and on what basis or bases?

36. How does the buyer secure information on current price changes on the raw-material and all intermediate markets?

37. Does the buyer utilize such information as may be available, and how does he use it?

38. Does the buyer make a systematic effort to secure information on price changes at all stages?

39. If such information were available to the buyer, would he utilize it, and how would he use it?

E. Ordering Practices

40. What is the average life of a contract?

41. What is the average annual number of purchases? of sales?

42. For a given time period, what is the average ratio of the number of purchases to the number of sales?

43. Do contracts ever call for staggered deliveries? If so, assuming that delivery dates and quantities are specified, are provisions ever made for prices on future deliveries to be revised at the time of each delivery?

44. Do such contracts ever carry escalator clauses or price-redetermination clauses?

45. Do suppliers insist on (a) large individual orders or (b) guarantees of minimum annual volume before extending prices and discounts corresponding to the annual volume of business?

46. Is it possible for the buyer to reorder a little at a time, in replacement of units sold, and still get favorable prices and discounts?

47. How frequently could the buyer reorder without taxing the ordering facilities or making the cost of handling such reorders prohibitive?

48. Indicate, for the more important classes of products, typical delivery times, from the date of mailing the order to the receipt of merchandise.

49. May orders be canceled?

F. Other Marketing Practices

50. What is, dollarwise, the approximate proportion of merchandise subject to manufacturer-suggested retail prices?

51. What is, dollarwise, the approximate proportion of merchandise otherwise subject to price fixing?

52. What is, dollarwise, the approximate proportion of merchandise purchased at flexible, fluid, often adjusted prices, versus rigid, pegged, stable prices?

53. Are the company's inventory levels essentially proportioned to requirements determined by delivery periods and average sales volumes?

54. Is the physical flow of merchandise from the raw-material producer to the consumer steady and even, or spasmodic and halting?

55. How does the buyer measure the supply-and-demand relationship?

Summary of Responses

A. General Character of the Establishment

1. The department store that volunteered to provide information for the survey is located in a large American city. Besides the main store located in the center of town, the firm operates about twenty suburban branches, which spill over into another market area. Total net assets, for all stores, amount to $250 million.

2. Annual sales, at the time of the survey, were $330 million.

3. One competing department store is larger in the primary market area, smaller if all market areas are included. Another is of comparable size.

4. Incomes of the clientele average $28,000 in the primary market area, and $21,800 in the remaining market area.

5. Ninety-five percent of the merchandise is procured directly from independent manufacturers, 5 percent from wholesalers or jobbers.

6. The company is affected by economic stagnation and instability.

7. The store has a problem of predicting the future consumer demand. Total demand has not fluctuated a great deal, but the product mix is difficult to anticipate. Furniture sales have fallen off with the purchase of new homes. Apparel has not changed appreciably.

8. The store is interested in solving these two problems.

9. The parent company has on its staff a group of economists. A firm of market-research consultants is retained to make regional forecasts; its predictions of optimum product mix are fairly accurate.

10. The main groups of departments are ladies' wear, thirteen departments; ladies' accessories, eight departments; men's and children's wear, five departments; and home furnishings, nine departments.

B. Degree of Vertical Specialization

11. The following sections (subdepartments) were included in the survey:

F = Living-room furniture section.

C = China, glassware, silverware section.

M = Misses' sportswear section.

12. F: Consecutive enterprises handling products range from three for lumber to eight for accessories. C: The number of stages is restricted. M: In ready-to-wear, there are four or five stages: the raw-fiber producer, the piece-goods manufacturer, the garment manufacturer, sometimes the wholesaler, and the retailer.

13. There is no compartmentalization of enterprises into independent divisions in the wholesale or retail business. M: Knitwear manufacturers often own their own finished yarn or piece-goods mills, which sell their output to the knitting mill for production into garments.

14. F: There are no examples of varying numbers of successive stages as between suppliers. C: Limited instances where the store imports foreign merchandise. M: Often a vendor contracts out the merchandise to be made by another firm, adding a stage.

15. F: The firm seeks to eliminate wholesalers, but that policy forces it to accumulate larger inventories. C: The establishment is not planning to increase the degree of vertical integration but mostly because, in the buyer's opinion, no advantage would be gained. M: In cases where the manufacturer is really an importer, it is possible to deal directly with the exporter.

16. The store is not considering mergers at the present time; this would hardly be practical.

   C. Proportion of Speculative Production and/or Distribution

17. F: Twenty-five percent of the merchandise is ordered for the customer, mainly couches and armchairs, because of the multiplicity of colors and designs in upholstery fabrics. C: The store always places a special order to accommodate a client. The proportion of business done on that basis is 25 percent. M: In ready-to-wear, an insignificant proportion of business is done as special orders. The store is not equipped to handle single-unit purchases.

18. F: Almost the totality of the merchandise is put in production after the store places its order. [This fact deserves to be noted.] C: Only 2 to 5 percent of imported porcelain dinnerware is manufactured to order; 0 percent of domestic merchandise. M: A very high percentage of ready-to-wear is made only after ordering. Over 60 percent of sweaters and knitwear are

imported, and these are not even designed until after receipt of an order. —All orders for custom-made goods are placed with independent manufacturers.

19. F: The proportion of merchandise put in production only after the retailer has received an order from the consumer is confined to that mentioned in answer to question 17. C and M: None.

20. F: The consumer does not have an opportunity to place advance orders at a saving. C: Import patterns can be ordered in advance but not at a saving. M: Styles and colors change too rapidly for placing advance orders.

21. F: The proportion of merchandise the selling price of which is revised to correspond to replacement prices varies with the product. C: Two methods are used: the manufacturer prescribes when and by how much prices are to be revised, so that all retailers in the area will have a coordinated price structure; for exclusive merchandise, revised prices are entered on old price tags the day the new merchandise is put on display. M: On seasonal goods, prices rarely go up. Normally there is a price reduction; the buyer then marks the merchandise at the regular price, subject to promotion later. Whenever the price goes up on a basic item kept in stock, the retail price is immediately increased, to maintain a constant markup structure.

22. Replacement prices are not consistently requested. C: New price lists are received at different intervals from different vendors. On imports, costs vary with the foreign currency and gold prices.

23. F: The buyer becomes aware of a price change only upon placing a new order; however, many prices are negotiable. M: Prices increase only with each new season (spring, summer, fall, holiday).

24. F: Circumstances dictate whether and when selling prices are revised. Merchandise is sold at the old price until a new shipment is received and put on display. C: Price lists ordinarily allow three to four weeks for the revision of price tags. Two organizational units handle price tags: the Marking Division prints them; the Re-Mark Division makes changes. M: Selling prices are revised immediately in line with new costs.

25. Will price lists be honored? Changes are infrequent, and ample notice is given the retailer. F: Many prices are subject to negotiation. M: Manufacturers do not raise prices after an order has been given.

26. Price lists are honored for 100 percent of the merchandise. In case of a price reduction, the store pays the lower price. F: Orders are placed with firm prices only. C: The buyer is not bound to accept a higher price. This applies to china and glassware but not to silverware. M: The merchandise

changes faster than price lists. The manufacturer simply applies a price on an item for the new season. Imported merchandise (25 to 30 percent of total) is ordered one year in advance; price trends for yarn and fabric, and business trends in the Orient, are watched to permit pricing competitively with domestic markets a year hence.

27. F: Price lists can be revised quickly. C: New price lists are sent twice a year, in January and July; between these dates, manufacturers mail supplements. Revisions can be in the hands of retailers within a week.

28. F: Price changes can be communicated promptly, even by telephone. C: The minimum time for relaying cost data would be one week.

D. Pricing Policy

29–35. F: With regard to the pricing policy, a good buyer anticipates the market about two months in advance. Prices are determined on the basis of anticipated changes on adjacent markets. The smart buyer also watches raw-material prices. [This identifies the speculative-pricing policy.] Most costs are firm for a negotiated period of time, generally six months or a year. Price breaks are frequent: during the year, manufacturers will offer short-term special deals. Or the store will approach suppliers for special pricing, special terms, and so forth. Selling prices are determined with the guidance of markup requirements for the department. C: Experience indicates that wholesale prices are fixed, denying the opportunity to apply a price policy. Prices do not change fast enough to require predictions. It is the policy of the store not to speculate on price movements. [This rules out the speculative-pricing policy in favor of the short-term pricing policy.] Occasionally stock is purchased at sale prices prior to a price increase to stage a special event. M: The speculative-pricing policy is used. There is even room for opportunism in importing goods; advantage is taken of favorable fluctuations in quotas and business trends in the Orient.—The synchronized-pricing policy is not used in the departments surveyed.

36–39. F: To obtain information on price changes at all stages, the buyer subscribes to industrial and commercial bulletins, such as periodicals on mattresses, rubber, cotton. The buyer must make connections, travel, see people. He develops relationships with fabric companies, follows changes in price, availability, and operations on the fabric market. Advertising funds are provided by fabric suppliers for use by the store. The buyer also works with furniture manufacturers to take advantage of price reductions. C: Inasmuch as the consumer must pay the asked price, there is no need to be concerned with raw-material prices other than to justify price rises. The only exception is gold, whose price has wild fluctuations and affects prices of goods containing it. M: Since price is the key to negotiations with manufacturers of ready-to-wear, the buyer's knowledge of the vendor's cost structure (piece-goods prices, importing costs, etc.) is important in getting the desired price. The better he is able to discuss ways the manufacturer can save his markup and still reduce the price, the better value the buyer will get. The buyer's relationship in the market and with corporate offices are keys to the knowledge he obtains. Foreign travel also helps clarify production costs of imports.

E. Ordering Practices

40. The contract used for the great majority of transactions consists of the manufacturer's purchase order and the store's written confirmation. Together the two agreements represent a legal instrument, binding on both parties. The purchase order and confirmation contain the following data in common: a serial number, the date, description of the merchandise, the quality, unit price, total price, terms of payment, shipping date, and destination. The manufacturer's purchase order specifies, in addition, the name of the salesman, that of the store, and the buyer. The confirmation omits these but adds the name of the manufacturer, the carrier to be used, and the date by which the complete order must be shipped. The life of the purchase order and confirmation combined extends over the period during which the order is filled, averaging about thirty days. An unconfirmed purchase order is not valid indefinitely. The manufacturer informs the buyer for how long prices will remain in effect. Conversely, if the manufacturer fails to meet the shipping date, the agreement is not necessarily canceled; it can always be extended. But the buyer retains the right to cancel if the merchandise is not on hand at the specified time.

41–42. F: Orders must be placed one month in advance. Quantities purchased must be adequate to last until replaced. The size of a single order varies with the value of the merchandise. High-priced sofas are bought in pairs, while inexpensive chairs are purchased by the thousand or five hundred. C: Stock purchases average three per month; special orders, one per day. Average purchases comprise 32 line units, or 128 pieces. M: For misses' knitwear, swimwear, and active wear, purchases are made on a daily basis, 20 to 100 purchase orders being placed monthly. The size of orders varies from 200 to 6,000 units, the average being 1,200 to 2,400 units.

43–44. F: Occasionally deliveries are staggered, but the price remains constant. C: Deliveries may be staggered, with quantities (not prices) adjusted before each shipment. With the exception of a possible reduction, prices are fixed. M: If deliveries are staggered, in domestic as well as foreign orders, the quoted price is maintained.

45. F: Among suppliers, some grant functional rebates or volume discounts. Others reduce prices based on item performance or on pure size of the account. Favorable prices are provided in some cases to secure a larger portion of the floor space. C: Most manufacturers now extend substantial discounts for large minimum quantities. M: In knitwear and active wear, price definitely changes with the quantity purchased and the timing of the order. Buying cuttings or buying when factories are slow helps reduce prices. Also, the later in the season, the lower the price.

46. Can the buyer order replacement units as the merchandise is sold without losing the discount? F: Yes. C: Generally reorders are accepted at the same discount. M: Usually the buyer reorders regardless of quantity, at the same or lower price. Seldom, however, does the buyer reorder less than the initial order.

47. F: With regard to the cost of reordering, it is negligible in the furniture department. The buyer can and does write special orders for each item; stocked items are reordered monthly. C: On orders costing under $100, a minimum-order charge is usually assessed. M: Reorders are usually placed as needed, based on the rate of sales, on expected sales, and on delivery times. Rarely is an item ordered more than once a month because of the time it takes to receive the merchandise and process it through the warehouse.

48. Typical delivery times are as follows. F: From two to sixteen weeks. C: Three to six weeks for domestic merchandise; three to six months for imports. M: For ready-to-wear, delivery times range from ten days to two months, with the bulk near thirty days. Initial orders, to test or start a season, are placed two to four months in advance. Imports are ordered a year in advance and reordered about four months ahead for delivery by airmail.

49. Are orders cancelable? F: Yes, until the merchandise is placed in production. C: All stock orders may be canceled unless they are part of an extra discount commitment. All special orders are cancelable, except import patterns. M: Cancellations are a matter subject to negotiation with the manufacturer. Most orders can be canceled if necessary. Special cuts and imports are cancelable only if the quality or delivery date is in question.

F. Other Marketing Practices

50–51. F: Other than for a few locally competitive items, the store generally determines its own selling prices. C: Eighty percent of the merchandise is sold at vendor-suggested (or vendor sale) prices. M: Swimwear is usually preticketed (90 percent); sweaters and active wear (0 percent). However, manufacturers will suggest retail prices if asked. Other than the above, prices are based by the store on the competitive market.

52. Price fluidity? F: Twenty percent of the prices are fluid, the balance, rigid. M: Domestically, 50 percent of the prices are fluid. The prices of initial orders are usually set. On sale orders, the percentage of savings is negotiated.

53. Inventory levels? F: Inventory levels generally reflect sales requirements. M: Sales projections govern inventory levels. Each week, adjustments are made based on sales trends. Stocks are related to quantities required.

54. Flow of merchandise? F: The flow of merchandise is spasmodic. C: The flow is generally continuous, with the exception of new products whose precise usage rate has not been established. M: The flow of goods to consumers is steady.

55. Supply and demand? C: The store is concerned mostly with its immediate demand, which dictates supply requirements. The future demand is anticipated from prior sales history and special order requests. The current sales trend helps to calculate increases in the demand.

Recommendations

The object of the diagnostic survey is to establish to what extent the department store may hope to benefit from the possible application of improved management and marketing methods. The specific policies presented in this book are designed to accomplish the liberation of the price mechanism from the many impediments to its free operation. The instant and accurate transmission of price fluctuations throughout the pipeline is to be assured, so that profit margins are allocated in balanced proportions to successive firms. Supply-and-demand flows will then tend to become synchronized and consumer wants to be met efficiently.

There exist mainly six approaches for achieving the desired results: vertical integration, production and distribution to order, the advance-order service, the replacement-pricing policy, the synchronized-pricing policy, and the open-price ordering policy. Several recommendations are proposed for the utilization of the policies.

Vertical Integration: No vertical mergers are contemplated by the store. But it seeks to eliminate wholesalers, although this necessitates the accumulation of larger inventories. In addition, variations exist between vendors with regard to the number of stages involved. Some manufacturers are really importers, and it is possible to deal directly with the exporter. Also knitwear manufacturers often own their own finished-yarn or piece-goods mills, which sell their output to the knitting mills for production into garments.

Recommendation 1: Avoid dealing with manufacturers that import foreign goods; buy directly from exporters. Also avoid vendors that subcontract the work to other firms.

Knitting mills and their subsidiaries are too far removed from the influence of the store to provide an opportunity for improvement.

Production and Distribution to Order: In the furniture department, almost all of the furniture is put in production after receipt of the store's order, and a very high percentage of ready-to-wear is likewise made to order. As far as it goes, this is favorable. The question is whether production to order can be expanded to include other important groups of products, such as china, glassware, and silverware, which are, almost without exception, produced speculatively. There may be overriding reasons why the present practices cannot easily be modified. However, it has not been known that production to order may have special merit; thus, in borderline cases, it might be well to examine opportunities for promoting that mode of operation. The store might attempt to exercise its influence on vendors and switch to those who comply with the advice.

The Advance-Order Service: Consumers do not have an opportunity to place advance orders at a saving. Of the three departments surveyed, the furniture department might have the best chances of success with the advance-order service. However, almost all of the furniture is already being produced to order, so little more would be gained through the service.

The Replacement-Pricing Policy: The replacement-pricing policy is only partially applied in the departments surveyed. Consequently it is advocated here for that merchandise not subject to controls by manufacturers.

Recommendation 2: Where the store has full control over retail prices, adopt the replacement-pricing policy. This means immediate revision of selling prices in line with replacement-cost changes as soon as these have come to the store's attention; also weekly or biweekly ordering of units in replacement of those sold, with the provision that no less than a predetermined minimum number of units be shipped at one time. Thus, the price the customer pays reflects current costs, and the physical flow of goods remains undisturbed. Allowances are made for seasonal goods.

The Synchronized-Pricing Policy: Furniture and misses' sportswear are bought and sold according to the speculative-pricing policy, and china according to the short-term pricing policy. Where the store has control over retail prices and where the replacement-pricing policy is not to be applied, the synchronized-pricing policy, reinforced by the open-price ordering policy, should be utilized by the store.

Recommendation 3: Where the store has control over retail prices and the replacement-pricing policy is not to be applied, it is recommended that the synchronized-pricing policy be substituted for the present policy.

The Open-Price Ordering Policy: That policy differs from the manufacturer's purchase order and the store's confirmation chiefly in the permanence of the purchase order and the frequency of partial confirmations. The necessary changes would thus not be substantial. An instrument is needed, in connection with the application of the synchronized-pricing policy, that will conveniently permit frequent reordering yet preserve maximum quantity discounts. The open-price ordering policy provides these features.

Recommendation 4: Wherever the synchronized-pricing policy is to be utilized, it is recommended that the ordering method be modified in keeping with the open-price ordering policy. It should permit frequent reordering without losing volume discounts.

These four recommendations should permit freer play of the price mechanism. The store has control only over its dealings with immediate vendors, but it can suggest to them similar modifications in relations with their suppliers. This may be helpful, and time might be well spent educating vendors and, through them, their suppliers. When the whole pipeline has been reached, positive results may be expected.

If the store's competitors should follow suit, this would in no way harm the store. Contrary to any other kind of innovation, which would intensify the pressure of competition, the recommended measures and policies, by recovering consumer purchasing power now going to waste, would ease the pressure for all who cater to the same market.

Conclusion

In a multistage economy, speculative production and distribution generate an economic entropy that may be unknown in a nonspeculative economy. The entropy is sufficient to explain general inefficiency in filling the consumer demand, economic stagnation leading to unemployment, economic instability leading to business cycles, and, together with political excesses, stagflation.

The entropy, or gap between the nation's production capacity and the effective consumer demand, has as its underlying microfoundation a partial paralysis of the principal self-adjustment mechanism of the economy: the price system. In a nonspeculative economy, price changes are freely transferable between markets, as had erroneously assumed Léon Walras for the real economy. The effect of speculative production and distribution is to place a number of critical obstacles in the path of vertical price change transfers.

As a result, supply and demand, while equated on each individual market, remain improperly matched when viewed through a vertical succession of markets. Furthermore, the very core of the economic process is disturbed. The profit motive, which is determined and allocated to successive firms by fluctuations of the price mechanism, is profoundly affected by the impediments to the free operation of that mechanism. Consequently the profit motive, acting as the mainspring and balance wheel of the whole economy, is chronically distorted; every signal received by every firm through its profit margin for every product is garbled. The entrepreneur who maximizes a garbled profit neither attains supply-and-demand equality, nor serves society best. These subjects are discussed in part I.

The entropy may not exist in a nonspeculative economy, however. Thus there may be a way out of confusion and inefficiency. It may be worthwhile investigating possibilities for avoiding the entropy altogether. If a nonspeculative economy is safe, perhaps modern equivalents of such an economy can be designed so that entrepreneurs might enjoy the best of two worlds: that preceding the Industrial Revolution and the modern world. Those are the topics explored in part II. The problem of economic entropy has received a theoretical explanation, and practical measures for avoiding the entropy are advocated for application by business.

Care was taken to reduce the extent of the changes to a minimum; as a result, they should be simple and inexpensive to apply. General application by a substantial segment of industry and commerce may take a generation. Eventually every entrepreneur will want to avail himself of sounder techniques for buying, selling, pricing, and ordering goods—and in the process increasing profits beyond levels now attainable. This should benefit producers, distributors, financiers, consumers, workers, investors, and government. No one should have to lose.

A better understanding of basic economic processes may lead to a vindication of the capitalist system, making possible the resolution of many national and international conflicts.

Bibliography

Aftalion, Albert. *Les crises périodiques de surproduction.* Paris: M. Rivière, 1913.

Arrow, Kenneth J.; Karlin, Samuel; and Scarf, Herbert. *Studies in the Mathematical Theory of Inventory and Production.* Stanford: Stanford University Press, 1958.

Arrow, Kenneth J., and Hahn, Frank H. *General Competitive Analysis.* San Francisco: Holden-Day, 1971.

Bell, Daniel, and Kristol, Irving, editors. *The Crisis in Economic Theory.* New York: Basic Books, 1981.

Beveridge, Sir William H. *Unemployment: a Problem of Industry.* London, New York: Longmans, Green, 1909, 1930; New York: AMS Press, 1969.

———. *Causes and Cures of Unemployment.* London, New York: Longmans, Green, 1931; New York: AMS Press, 1976.

———. *Full Employment in a Free Society.* London: G. Allen & Unwin, 1944; New York: W.W. Norton, 1945.

Boulding, Kenneth E. *Economic Analysis.* New York and London: Harper, 1941, 1955; New York: Harper & Row, 1966.

———. *Economics as a Science.* New York: McGraw-Hill, 1970.

———. *Ecodynamics: a New Theory of Societal Evolution.* Beverly Hills: Sage Publications, 1978.

Bouniatian, Mentor. *Les crises économiques.* Paris: M. Giard, 1922, 1930.

———. *Les fluctuations économiques: recueil d'études.* Paris: R. Pichon et R. Durand-Auzias, 1959.

Bovet, Eric D. "Fresh Study of Profit Motive Aimed at Economic Stability." *Christian Science Monitor,* January 3, 1945.

———. *L'organisation rationnelle de la distribution, moyen de stabilisation économique.* Neuchâtel, Switzerland, and Paris, France: Delachaux & Niestlé, 1954.

———. "La mesure du rapport entre l'offre et la demande—Technique utile à l'étude des causes profondes des crises." *Kyklos,* no. 4 (1955).

———. *The Dynamics of Business Motivation—Its Impact on the Economic Climate.* Washington, D.C.: Spartan Books, 1963.

Cassell, Gustav. *The Theory of Social Economy.* London: T.F. Unwin, 1923; New York: A.M. Kelley, 1967.

Chamberlain, Edward H. *The Theory of Monopolistic Competition.* Cambridge: Harvard University Press, 1933, 1976.

Clark, John M. *Studies in the Economics of Overhead Costs.* Chicago: University of Chicago Press, 1923.

———. *Strategic Factors in Business Cycles.* New York: H. Wolff, 1934.

Clower, Robert W., and Leijonhufvud, Axel. *Income, Employment and Monetary Theory.* Santa Monica: BFA Educational Media, 1974.

Davidson, Paul, and Smolensky, Eugene. *Aggregate Supply-and-Demand Analysis.* New York: Harper & Row, 1964.

———. *Money and the Real World.* New York: Wiley, 1972; London: Macmillan, 1972.

Drucker, Peter F. *Toward the Next Economics, and Other Essays.* New York: Harper & Row, 1974.

———. *Management: Tasks, Responsibilities, Practices.* New York: Harper & Row, 1974.

———. *Effective Management Performance.* London: British Institute of Management, 1978.

———. *Managing in Turbulent Times.* New York: Harper & Row, 1980.

Fisher, Irving. *Booms and Depressions, Some First Principles.* New York: Adelphi, 1932.

———. "The Debt-Deflation Theory of Great Depressions." *Econometrica* (October 1933).

Foster, William T., and Catchings, Waddill. *Money.* Boston: Houghton Mifflin, 1923.

———. *Profits.* Boston: Houghton Mifflin, 1925.

———. *Progress and Plenty.* Newton, Mass.: Pollak Foundation for Economic Research, 1930.

Galbraith, John K. *American Capitalism: The Concept of Countervailing Power.* Boston: Houghton Mifflin, 1952; White Plains, N.Y.: M.E. Sharpe, 1980.

———. *A Theory of Price Control.* Cambridge: Harvard University Press, 1952, 1980.

———. *The Affluent Society.* Boston: Houghton Mifflin, 1958, 1976.

———. *The New Industrial State.* Boston: Houghton Mifflin, 1967.

———. *The Age of Uncertainty.* Boston: Houghton Mifflin, 1977.

Haberler, Gottfried. *Prosperity and Depression: A Theoretical Analysis of Cyclical Movements.* Geneva: League of Nations, 1937; Cambridge: Harvard University Press, 1958.

Hahn, Frank H. *On the Notion of Equilibrium in Economics: An Inaugural Lecture.* London: Cambridge University Press, 1973.

———, and Hollis, Martin. *Philosophy and Economic Theory.* New York: Oxford University Press, 1979.

Harrod, Roy F. *The Trade Cycle.* Oxford: Oxford University Press, 1936.

Hawtrey, Ralph G. *Currency and Credit.* London, New York: Longmans, Green, 1919, 1950; New York: Arno Press, 1979.

———. *Trade and Credit.* London, New York: Longmans, Green, 1928.

———. *Trade Depression and the Way Out.* London, New York: Longmans, Green, 1931.

———. *The Art of Central Banking.* London, New York: Longmans, Green,

1932; London: F. Cass, 1962.

———. *Capital and Employment.* London, New York: Longmans, Green, 1937, 1951.

———. *Economic Destiny.* London, New York: Longmans, Green, 1944.

———. *Economic Rebirth.* London, New York: Longmans, Green, 1946.

Hayek, Friedrich A. *Prices and Production.* London: G. Routledge, 1931; New York: A.M. Kelley, 1967.

———. *Monetary Theory and the Trade Cycle.* New York: Harcourt, Brace, 1933; New York: A.M. Kelley, 1966.

———. *Profits, Interest, and Investment, and Other Essays on the Theory of Industrial Fluctuations.* London: G. Routledge, 1939; New York: A.M. Kelley, 1969.

———. *The Pure Theory of Capital.* London: Macmillan, 1941.

———. *The Road to Serfdom.* London: G. Routledge; Chicago: University of Chicago Press, 1944.

———. "The Use of Knowledge in Society." *American Economic Review* (September 1945): 519–530.

———. *Individualism and Economic Order.* Chicago: University of Chicago Press, 1948; London: Routledge and K. Paul, 1949; Chicago: H. Regnery, 1972.

———. *A Tiger by the Tail: A Forty-Years' Running Commentary on Keynesianism by Hayek.* Compiled by Sudha R. Shenoy. London: Institute of Economic Affairs, 1972.

———. *Full Employment at Any Price?* London: Institute of Economic Affairs, 1975.

———. *Choice in Currency: A Way to Stop Inflation.* London: Institute of Economic Affairs, 1976.

Hicks, Sir John R. *A Contribution to the Theory of the Trade Cycle.* Oxford: Clarendon Press, 1950.

———. *The Crisis in Keynesian Economics.* Oxford: Blackwell, 1974; New York: Basic Books, 1975.

Hobson, John A. *The Industrial System.* London, New York: Longmans, Green, 1909; New York: A.M. Kelley, 1969.

———. *The Economics of Unemployment.* London: G. Allen & Unwin, 1922.

———. *Rationalisation and Unemployment.* London: G. Allen & Unwin; New York: Macmillan, 1930.

Kaldor, Nicholas. *Essays on Economic Stability and Growth.* London: G. Duckworth; Glencoe, Ill.: Free Press, 1960; New York: Holmes & Meier, 1980.

———. "The Irrelevance of Equilibrium Economics." *Economic Journal* (December 1972): 1237–1255.

———. *Further Essays on Economic Theory.* New York: Holmes & Meier, 1978.

Keynes, John M. *Treatise on Money.* New York: Macmillan, 1930.

————. *The General Theory of Unemployment, Interest and Money.* London: Macmillan; New York: Harcourt, Brace, 1936.

Knight, Frank H. *Risk, Uncertainty and Profit.* Boston: Kelley, 1921.

Kornai, Janos. *Anti-Equilibrium: On Economic Systems Theory and the Tasks of Research.* New York: American Elsevier; Amsterdam and London: North Holland, 1971.

————. *Pressure and Suction on the Market.* Bloomington: Indiana University Press, 1971.

————. *Economics of Shortage.* Stockholm: Institute for International Economic Studies, University of Stockholm, 1979.

Kuznets, Simon S. *Economic Change: Selected Essays in Business Cycles, National Income, and Economic Growth.* New York: W.W. Norton, 1953.

Lederer, Emil. *Technical Progress and Unemployment: An Inquiry into the Obstacles to Economic Expansion.* Geneva, Switzerland: International Labor Office, 1938.

Leijonhufvud, Axel E. *On Keynesian Economics and the Economics of Keynes: A Study in Monetary Theory.* New York: Oxford University Press, 1968.

————. *Keynes and the Classics: Two Lectures on Keynes' Contribution to Economic Theory.* London: Institute of Economic Affairs, 1969.

Machlup, Fritz. *The Stock Market, Credit and Capital Formation.* London: W. Hodge, 1940.

————. *The Economics of Sellers' Competition: Model Analysis of Sellers' Conduct.* Baltimore: Johns Hopkins Press, 1952.

————. *The Production and Distribution of Knowledge in the U.S.* Princeton: Princeton University Press, 1962.

Malthus, Thomas R. *An Essay on the Principle of Population, as It Affects the Future Improvement of Society.* London: J. Johnson, 1798.

Marshall, Alfred. *Principles of Economics.* London and New York: Macmillan, 1890, 1961.

Marx, Karl. *Das Kapital.* Hamburg: O. Meissner; New York: L.W. Schmidt, 1867.

Mill, John S. *Principles of Political Economy, with Some of Their Applications to Social Philosophy.* London: Longmans, 1848.

Mises, Ludwig von. *Geldwertstabilisierung und Konjunkturpolitik.* Jena: G. Fischer, 1928.

————. *The Theory of Money and Credit.* London: J. Cape, 1934; New Haven: Yale University Press, 1953.

————. *Economic Planning.* New York: Dynamic America, 1945.

————. *Human Action, A Treatise on Economics.* New Haven: Yale University Press; London: W. Hodge, 1949.

Mitchell, Thomas W. "Competitive Illusion as a Cause of Business Cycles."

Quarterly Journal of Economics 38 (August 1924).

Mitchell, Wesley C. *Business Cycles*. Berkeley: University of California Press, 1913; New York: B. Franklin, 1970.

———. *Business Cycles, the Problem and Its Setting*. New York: National Bureau of Economic Research, 1927; New York: Arno Press, 1975.

———. *Business Cycles and Their Causes*. Berkeley: University of California Press, 1941.

———. *What Happens during Business Cycles: A Progress Report*. New York: National Bureau of Economic Research, 1951.

Mitchell, Wesley C., and Arthur F. Burns. *Measuring Business Cycles*. New York: National Bureau of Economic Research, 1946.

Nordhaus, William D. "The Falling Share of Profits." *Brookings Papers on Economic Activity* 1 (1974).

Okun, Arthur M. *Unemployment*. New York: W.W. Norton, 1965.

———. *The Political Economy of Prosperity*. New York: W.W. Norton, 1970.

———. "Notes and Numbers on the Profits Squeeze." *Brookings Papers on Economic Activity* 3 (1970).

———, and Perry, George L. *Curing Chronic Inflation*. Washington, D.C.: Brookings Institute, 1978.

Pareto, Vilfredo. *Cours d'économie politique*. Lausanne: F. Rouge; Paris: Pichon, 1896. Translated as *Manual of Political Economy*. New York: A.M. Kelley, 1971.

Pigou, Arthur C. *Industrial Fluctuations*. London: Macmillan, 1927; New York: A.M. Kelley, 1967.

———. *The Theory of Unemployment*. London: Macmillan, 1933; New York: A.M. Kelley, 1968.

———. *Employment and Equilibrium: A Theoretical Discussion*. London: Macmillan, 1941; Fairfield, N.J.: A.M. Kelley, 1978.

———. *Lapses from Full Employment*. London: Macmillan, 1945; Fairfield, N.J.: A.M. Kelley, 1977.

Ricardo, David. *On the Principles of Political Economy and Taxation*. London: J. Murray, 1817; Harmondsworth: Penguin, 1971.

Robinson, Joan. *The Economics of Imperfect Competition*. London: Macmillan, 1933, 1969.

———. *Essays in the Theory of Employment*. New York: Macmillan, 1937.

———. *Economic Heresies: Some Old-Fashioned Questions in Economic Theory*. London: Macmillan; New York: Basic Books, 1971.

———. *The Generalization of the General Theory*. New York: St. Martin's Press, 1979.

Rueff, Jacques. *From the Physical to the Social Sciences*. Baltimore: The Johns Hopkins Press, 1929.

Samuelson, Paul A. *Economics, an Introductory Analysis*. New York: McGraw-Hill, 1948, 1980.

———, and Burns, Arthur F. *Full Employment: Guideposts and Economic*

Stability. Washington, D.C.: American Enterprise Institute for Public Policy Research, 1967.

Say, Jean-Baptiste. *Traité d'économie politique.* Paris: Deterville, 1803; Paris: Calmann-Lévy, 1972. Translated as *A Treatise on Political Economy.* Boston: Wells & Lilly, 1821; Philadelphia: Claxton, Rensen & Haffelfinger, 1880; New York: A.M. Kelley, 1964.

Schumpeter, Joseph A. *The Theory of Economic Development: An Inquiry into Profits, Capital, Credit, Interest, and the Business Cycle.* Cambridge: Harvard University Press, 1934.

———. *Business Cycles: A Theoretical, Historical, and Statistical Analysis of the Capitalist Process.* New York: McGrath, 1939.

Smith, Adam. *An Inquiry into the Nature and Causes of the Wealth of Nations.* London: W. Strahan & Cadell, 1776; Chicago: University of Chicago Press, 1976.

Spiethoff, Arthur A.C. *Die wirtschaftlichen Wechsellagen: Aufschwung, Krise, Stockung.* Tubingen: Mohr, 1955.

Sraffa, Piero. *Production of Commodities by Means of Commodities.* Cambridge: Cambridge University Press, 1960.

Taussig, Frank W. *Principles of Economics.* New York: Macmillan, 1911, 1939.

Walras, Léon. *Eléments d'économie politique pure.* Lausanne: L. Corbaz, 1874; Paris: Librairie générale de droit et de jurisprudence, 1952. Translated as *Elements of Pure Economics.* London: Allen & Unwin, 1954.

Weintraub, Sidney. *A General Theory of the Price Level, Output, Income Distribution, and Economic Growth.* Philadelphia: Chilton, 1959.

Wicksell, Knut. *Lectures on Political Economy.* London: G. Routledge, 1934.

———. *Interest and Prices.* London: Macmillan, 1936.

Index

About the Author

Eric D. Bovet obtained the Ph.D. and the M.B.A. from the University of Geneva. He has taught at Columbia University and The University of Colorado, Boulder. His publications include a book on economic theory and preventive remedies.